THE AFTER-WORLD
OF THE POETS

THE AFTER-WORLD OF THE POETS

THE CONTRIBUTION OF VICTORIAN POETS TO THE DEVELOPMENT OF THE IDEA OF IMMORTALITY

By
LESLIE D. WEATHERHEAD

KENNIKAT PRESS
Port Washington, N. Y./London

THE AFTER-WORLD OF THE POETS

First published in 1929
Reissued in 1970 by Kennikat Press
Library of Congress Catalog Card No: 71-105848
ISBN 0-8046-1058-4

Manufactured by Taylor Publishing Company   Dallas, Texas

TO
MY TEACHER AND FRIEND

PROFESSOR H. B. CHARLTON, M.A.
(Professor of English Literature in the
University of Manchester)

WHO TAUGHT ME HOW TO APPRECIATE
ENGLISH POETRY.

In gratitude and esteem.

CONTENTS

CHAP.		PAGE
	PREFACE	9
I.	THE VALIDITY OF THE POET'S CONTRIBUTION TO IDEAS	11
II.	THE DISCARDING OF ORTHODOX IDEAS OF IMMORTALITY	31
	1 Wordsworth	
	2 Shelley	
III.	A NEW PROJECTION OF CHRISTIAN THOUGHT BORN OF THE FEAR OF DEATH	79
	Tennyson	
IV.	THE CONTRIBUTION OF DOUBT	123
	1 Arnold	
	2 Clough	
	3 Swinburne	
V.	THE CLIMAX OF DEVELOPMENT	171
	Browning	
VI.	CONCLUSION	221
	INDEX	225

FOREWORD

It is with pleasure that I write a brief Introduction to this volume. I have a warm regard for the author himself and a cordial admiration for his gifts. That if life and health are granted him he has before him a distinguished career in the ministry I do not doubt. But I am the more confident because he has not yielded to the temptation to stake his future on his talent for popular speech. He has recognized the duty of strenuous study and hard thinking.

The problem of the after-life had previously engaged his attention; and it was a fortunate inspiration which led him to choose as an academic task the conception of man's destiny after death entertained by some of our Victorian poets. The material has been collected and classified with great care and industry, and presented in a convenient form for which many of his readers will be grateful. His fellow-craftsmen in particular will, I believe, welcome not only the author's own felicitous exposition but the illustrative quotation which is supplied in such fullness.

That he should devote such loving study to poets of the Victorian era will, I trust, be counted to him for righteousness. Those of us who have a long life behind us have, with all our drawbacks, at least enjoyed the advantages of a wide experience. We have observed that the standard of values is constantly shifting and that literary idolatries have often but a fleeting vogue. The cynicism with which we listen to the depreciation of the great Victorians will, we do not doubt, be justified by the impartial verdict of history.

The theme which Mr. Weatherhead has chosen is one

FOREWORD

of the deepest interest. That the belief in survival may at times fall into the background, and even become the object of bitter criticism, does not alter the fact that the human spirit swings back to this magnetic pole. For it the Christian Church is pledged to stand without flinching; a belief in immortality is involved in our conception of God as revealed to us in Christ.

I have read this book with deep interest and real refreshment of spirit and trust it may find a wide circle of readers.

ARTHUR S. PEAKE.

February 21, 1929.

PREFACE

WHEN I was writing my book entitled *After Death*, published five years ago by James Clarke & Co., I was very much impressed by one fact. I discovered that the most modern theological conceptions concerning the life beyond the grave, conceptions which I expressed in that book and which caused me considerable trouble when the book was published, were almost all contained in the poetry of the Victorians. It was significant that Tennyson and Browning had expressed over fifty years ago views for which a theologian would even now be dubbed modernist or even heretic.

I therefore determined that a most interesting hobby-study would be to work out what actually is the contribution of Victorian poetry to the idea of immortality, and I approached Professor Peake, for whose advice and wise guidance, and, further, for whose kindness in writing a foreword to this volume, I can never adequately express my gratitude.

Living near the University of Manchester, it became possible for me to study there and to have access to the University Library. But of far greater assistance than any library were the interviews with Professor Alexander, a philosopher of European reputation, the philosophy lectures of Dr. Roth, and most of all the lectures of, and personal interviews with, Professor Charlton.

Professor Charlton for a period of three years supervised my studies, guided my reading, helped me to form judgements, and opened the door into a new world for me, a world of wonder and delight. I shall count it one of the privileges of my life to have known him and to have gained such permanent enrichment from him.

Most of the chapters of the book have appeared in summarized form as articles in *The London Quarterly Review*. The first chapter appeared in a modified form in *The Holborn Review*. The matter has all been rewritten, but I am grateful to the editors of both these journals, Mr. Telford and Dr. Peake, for permission to reprint. I must also express my gratitude to my beloved father-in-law, the Rev. Arthur Triggs, who once more has helped me prepare the book for the press; and, not least, to my accomplished friend and secretary, Miss Margaret Webster, for checking the quotations and proof-corrections and for preparing the Index.

L. D. W.

I

THE VALIDITY OF THE POET'S
CONTRIBUTION TO IDEAS

'It appears to me, Socrates, probably as it does to you with respect to these matters, that to know them clearly in the present life is either impossible, or very difficult: on the other hand, however, not to test what has been said of them in every possible way, so as not to desist until, on examining them in every point of view, one has exhausted every effort, is the part of a very weak man.'

Plato, *Phaedo*, 85.

The After-World of the Poets

I

THE VALIDITY OF THE POET'S CONTRIBUTION TO IDEAS

BEFORE any attempt is made to estimate the contribution of the poet to any specific philosophic idea, there are certain preliminary questions which ought to be considered. We must ask what we mean by a poetical idea. We must ask whether ideas are the concern of the poet. We must ask how he arrives at his conceptions, and what their value is when arrived at. If we are to discuss a philosophic or religious idea, would it not be more reasonable to confine our investigations to the philosopher or the theologian, both of whom set out with the specific intention of arriving, as far as man may, at truth ; or, at any rate, of contributing ideas which aid man's quest for truth ?

I

To begin at the beginning, we must ask what we mean by the idea of a poet. It would be a gross mistake to pick out an idea in a haphazard manner from a poem and say that it was a contribution by the poet to the ideas of the world. In theological and philosophical works this mistake has frequently been made in quoting from the poets. Browning, for instance, because so much of his poetry deals with philosophic ideas, has been greatly misused in this way ; yet the quoted words may be the words of Browning, or the words, say, of Paracelsus, or the words of a poet *qua* poet. Mrs. Olwen Ward Campbell has pointed out, in her book on Shelley,[1] that he is quoted by theist and atheist; by philosophers who find he illustrates abstruse theories, and by aesthetes who declare his work to be a fine illustration of art for art's sake; by democrats and socialists; not to mention vegetarians, Mormons, and spiritualists.

We must be careful, then, lest we are betrayed into supposing that a poet supports a view or an idea we would dearly like to believe, simply because some few lines of his poetry appear—or can be distorted—to support it.

We must also be on our guard against accepting an idea as one which the poet really does give to the world, stamped with the image and superscription of his own personality, simply because it occurs a certain number of times in his poems. Room must be made for the fact that even a poet is not inspired every time he writes. As Coleridge says, ' A poem of any length neither can be nor ought to be all poetry.' A poet often copies inspired poems. He often writes conventionally.

> 'Tis not every day that I
> Fitted am to prophesy,

sings Herrick. The danger we are anxious to avoid can be illustrated from Swinburne. Consider the idea of immortality. If the number of times this subject is referred to in Swinburne be reckoned up, and divided, according as he supports the idea or denies it, it will be found that he supports it in far more poems than he denies it. This is due to the fact that he wrote a great number of memorial verses, which can be described as conventional. But, as we shall see, it would be inaccurate to deduce from this that Swinburne believed in the immortality of the soul. His *best* poetry supports

[1] *Shelley and the Unromantics*, p. 2.

the conclusion, which other evidence confirms, that he denied it.

Before we can say that a certain idea is held by a certain poet we must read the whole of his poems. We must track that idea through them, while still reading them as poems. If we find that in various kinds of poems, written in various moods, in various places, a certain idea persists; if, again and again, it bursts forth, passionately inspiring lyrical utterance and giving birth to song, rather than to argument; then we may conclude that it has been taken up, not as a mental toy, by the poet, but that he has accepted it as what Professor Dowden has called 'a truth of the emotions.'

2

But another preliminary question suggests itself. Is it the poet's concern to contribute to the ideas of the world? Is it his business to inculcate them? We think it important to state emphatically that it is not the primary interest of the poet either to inculcate philosophic ideas or to give to the world ethical teaching. The functions of poetry and morality, Aristotle asserted, have nothing in common. We shall be led to deal later, however briefly and inadequately, with the sources of poetical inspiration; but, whatever motive the poet has, it certainly is not didactic. 'Didactic poetry,' bursts out Shelley in the Preface to 'Prometheus Unbound,' 'is my abhorrence.'

The poet writes, not to give the world ideas or to teach it lessons, but simply because he is moved by an inward compulsion which urges him to creative art. (ποιητής—creator.) 'Sing I must, else life's not life,' Goethe makes Tasso say. 'My passions raged like so many devils,' writes Burns in a letter, 'till they got vent in rhyme.' 'Poetry is the lava of the imagination whose eruption prevents the earthquake,' says Byron; and Wordsworth speaks of the relief accorded to him by ' a timely utterance.'

If the poet can be said to have a motive, then it is aesthetic desire. If he can be said to have a purpose, it is to give pleasure. In some moment of poetic insight he has seen a vision of the infinite, and he craves so to express that experience that it may be shared with those who, with seeing eyes and understanding hearts, read his poetry. ' All poetry,' said Browning, ' is the problem of getting the infinite into the finite.' Poetry has lost in two ways when its motive has been mistakenly thought to be didactic. It has lost what it exists to give the reader, when he has read it simply in order to wrest from it either philosophical ideas or ethical teaching. It has lost its *raison d'être* to the poet when he has misused it to make it an instrument for the dissemination of his views, and allowed the didactic to preponderate over the aesthetic. May we not say that poetry is misunderstood and misused unless it is written as poetry, read as poetry, and loved for its own sake?

'Tis you speak, that's your error, song's our art,

says the poet in ' Transcendentalism '; though it may be said that Browning himself, in some later poems, fell into that very error, and allowed the bones of his doctrine to protrude somewhat gauntly through the fair flesh of certain poems. And if we are more conscious that we are being harangued than that we are reading a beautiful poem, we may conclude that there is some degree of failure in artistry.

The pictures of Watts form an interesting parallel in a sister art. They nearly all teach some allegorical or ethical lesson; but the didactic motive is subordinated to the aesthetic. We enter into truth, perhaps, but through the door of beauty. We do not so much learn; we see. Thousands of people have hung on

POET'S CONTRIBUTION TO IDEAS

their walls copies of 'Hope.' Probably only one in a hundred could explain its meaning or teaching. It is beautiful, and that is reason enough for it to be hung. Moreover, there is something 'felt,' of which ordinary folk are conscious, but which they cannot explain. Watts has not taught them much. He has given them something beautiful, and they dimly *feel* his meaning. So Arnold, in his 'Memorial Verses,' says of Byron :

> When Byron's eyes were shut in death,
> We bow'd our head and held our breath.
> He taught us little ; but our soul
> Had *felt* him like the thunder's roll.

Keats illustrates our point admirably when he says that a poet should have no opinions, no principles, no morality, no self. 'To be tied to these things spoils true art, which should be entirely unfettered. The poet should make a clean sweep of his personal hopes, enthusiasms, and beliefs.' Keats was so desirous of being the consummate artist that he did not want private ideas and ethical principles to spoil his poems, as the wire support of the florist sometimes spoils the beauty of the natural curve in the stem of a flower. He wanted to present his poem just as it came to him from God. 'All poets who have forgotten themselves in the theme of their flights of fancy have, when engaged in production, to the best of their ability banished their private peculiarities and preferences. Few have managed to make such a clean sweep as Keats of their personal hopes, enthusiasms, and principles. His study was, as one of his admirers has said, " a painter's studio with very little in it besides the easel." '[1]

Of course, the poet has to work with words as his medium, and the words are bound to express ideas ; but those ideas should be poetic—the ideas received

[1] George Brandes, *Main Currents in Nineteenth Century Literature*, vol. iv., p. 138.

BP

by poetic insight, not the personal opinions of a private individual. Thus Mr. Chesterton objects that 'the great fault of most of the appreciation of Browning lies in the fact that it conceives the moral and artistic value of his work to lie in what is called " the message of Browning," or " the teaching of Browning," or, in other words, " in the mere opinions of Browning." '[1] One does not so much want to learn what Browning's private opinions were. One wants to know what Browning saw in his hours of poetic vision, and one wants to see through his eyes.

We should therefore be guarded in speaking of the ' value ' of the work of the poet, just as we should speak guardedly of the ' value ' of a sunset, or one of Turner's pictures, or one of Chopin's nocturnes. As Tennyson says :

> So, Lady Flora, take my lay,
> And if you find no moral there,
> Go, look in any glass and say,
> What moral is in being fair.
> Oh, to what uses shall we put
> The wild weed-flower that simply blows ?
> And is there any moral shut
> Within the bosom of the rose ?
>
> But any man that walks the mead,
> In bud or blade, or bloom, may find,
> According as his humours lead,
> A meaning suited to his mind.
> And liberal applications lie
> In Art like Nature, dearest friend ;
> So 'twere to cramp its use, if I
> Should hook it to some useful end.

That the poet is a teacher in one sense we shall see. But he is not the pedagogue. He is the artist, the dreamer, the visionary, and he exists, not to inculcate ideas as the teacher, but to reveal reality.

[1] *Robert Browning* (' English Men of Letters '), p. 177.

3

Our third preliminary question must be concerning the way in which the poet arrives at his conceptions. Obviously, before we can determine the validity of the poet's contribution to ideas we must ask how he arrives at them. Are they the product of a mental process different from that of others?

We can say, first of all, that a poet does not reach the ideas expressed in his best poetry by a method of logical argument. He is not sure of a truth because he has proved it, but because he has seen it. Indeed, in some moments of rapture he has experienced it, and henceforth he is a 'dedicated spirit,' ordained to give it, by means of poetry, to the world, as far as the infinite can be expressed in finite language; for Shelley has warned us that 'the most glorious poetry that has ever been communicated to the world is probably a feeble shadow of the original conceptions of the poet.'[1]

The poet is, therefore, untroubled if his ideas cannot be fitted into some logical scheme of thought, or if he expresses an idea at one time which appears inconsistent with an idea expressed at another time. He is not upset if the philosopher challenges his ideas. They are indubitable to him, not as the conclusion of a theorem of Euclid is indubitable, but as the beauty of a summer dawn is indubitable. And the poet must be judged, not by the standards of any science, but by the standards of art. His work is never ratiocinative—unless, of course, he is artistically representing a ratiocinative person. It is not necessarily ethical. It is intuitive. In an ultimate philosophical sense it may or may not be found that the truth is beautiful, and the beautiful true, and both ethical; yet there are three distinct points of view.

We have said that the poet 'sees,' that his ideas are

[1] Shelley, *Defence of Poetry*, p. 53.

'intuitive.' What does this mean? It is sometimes thought that the poetic mode of arriving at truth is only different in degree from the normal mode of thinking. We believe this conclusion to be erroneous. We believe that the poet arrives at his ideas by a mental operation entirely different in kind from that, say, of the logicians. Without taking the space to go into the matter completely, we believe that we must look for the source of the poet's conceptions in the same direction whence come to us those of the dreamer, the visionary, the mystic. 'The true poet dreams, being awake,' says Charles Lamb. He is in the same category with Bunyan, with the author of the Revelation of St. John, with Sadhu Sundar Singh, with St. Francis of Assisi, and a thousand more. He arrives at truth, as Shelley says in 'Alastor,'

> By solemn vision, and bright silver dream.

This does not mean, of course, that his mind always works in this manner. Like other men, he can use either mode of thinking; but, unlike other men, his moments of vision are far more frequent, far more vivid, and, above all, though all men dream at times, the poet can tell his dream and share it with others.

> Every man whose soul is not a clod
> Hath visions;

but

> Poesy alone can tell her dreams.[1]

Aristotle, in the *Poetics*, believed poetry to be inspired, and to imply 'either a strain of madness or a happy gift of nature'; and he divides poetry into the ecstatic and the euplastic. It is the ecstatic poet with

---

[1] Keats, 'Hyperion.'

POET'S CONTRIBUTION TO IDEAS 21

whom we are concerned, for he alone requires explanation. Yet the word we have used is, in part, an explanation. The poet, inspired by some vivid experience, goes into a kind of trance[1]—we think the phrase is not too strong—and thereupon sees a vision which he expresses in poetical ideas, that those who read may have that experience re-created in them. It was to such a moment, we think, that Wordsworth referred in the lines addressed to his sister on ' the first mild day of March ' :

> One moment now may give us more
> Than years of toiling reason.

It is because of this different way of arriving at truth, we think, that the poet has so often led the way in expressing ideas which are among the most profound cherished by mankind. On the wings of vision the poet soars to a pinnacle of truth. The theologian or philosopher creeps upon the ground, hindered by many an obstacle, by many a crevice of thought. It is a matter of fact that the more important speculations concerning the life after death, which are being hesitantly accepted by the ultra-modern school of theologians to-day, may all be found expressed both by Tennyson and Browning. This, it seems to us, is part of the glory of poetry. It often gives us truths which reason cannot give and at which it dare not guess. It thus stimulates research by showing us the goal of certain lines of inquiry, lest we grow faint-hearted in pursuing them. Some philosophers would say, with Stevenson, ' To travel hopefully is better than to arrive ' ; but the poets would say, with Carlyle, that ' the end of understanding is not to prove and find reasons, but to know and

---

[1] Cf. Tennyson :
' At length my trance
Was cancell'd, stricken thro' with doubt.'
' In Memoriam,' xcv. 43-4.

believe.' 'To the poets,' says Professor Harper,[1] 'and to Wordsworth more than to other poets, belongs a faculty for discovering those precious yet subtle truths, which the net of reason is too coarse to touch.' It will be remembered that Wordsworth prayed for this gift in the Preface to 'The Excursion':

> Upon me bestow
> A gift of genuine insight.

Although, as we shall endeavour to show in the next paragraph, the poet arrives at his ideas by a legitimate and valid mode of thought, yet what we have called his state of trance is often so profound that he himself can scarcely believe that the ideas he expresses have risen from within. With Voltaire he cries, 'Was it really I who wrote that?' In this the poets are one with the biblical writers who ascribed their ideas to God. Isaiah says, 'The word of the Lord came unto me, saying ...' Browning says:

> God has a few of us whom He whispers in the ear.

The way of arriving at truth is the same; the 'inspiration' is the same in quality in both cases; nor does it matter for our purpose here that the Hebrew speaks of God, that the Greek speaks of the muse, that Milton speaks of a 'celestial patroness,' or that Wordsworth cries:

> Descend, prophetic spirit! that inspir'st
> The human Soul of universal earth,
> Dreaming on things to come.[2]

The point is that in poetry we have an entirely different way of arriving at certain conceptions from that of the

---

[1] *William Wordsworth*, vol. ii., p. 225.
[2] Preface to 'The Excursion.' Cf. also Shakespeare's Sonnet 107.

logician; a way in which the conscious mind seems to play but a small part, and in which the difference is so great that the ideas seem to come from without. Mozart would say that this is true also of music. Emerson would say that this view applies to all art:

> Himself from God he could not free;
> He builded better than he knew.
>
> . . . .
>
> The passive Master lent his hand
> To the vast soul that o'er him planned.

But into the wider issue we need not enter. The view holds at any rate for the poets.

> So come to the Poet his songs
> All hitherward blown
> From the misty realm that belongs
> To the vast Unknown.
>
> His, and not his, are the lays
> He sings.[1]

We are conscious that we have not explained the poet's way of arriving at his conceptions. Poetry, as Shelley said, 'acts in a divine and unapprehended manner, beyond and above consciousness.' The explanation lies with the psychologist, who, as far as we are aware, has never rationalized the mental processes of the poet.

The springs of poetical creative art may be in the unconscious mind, which is being explored so busily by the modern psychologist. It may be that the poet, in certain moods, can, by what we call imagination, stimulated by emotion, tap those depths wherein the experiences of the past lie buried. It may be that the poet's creation is actually of the substance of the dream, and so—if the Freudian hypothesis be accepted

[1] Longfellow, 'L'Envoi.'

—may point to some as yet unrealized desire of humanity, for which the poet, as a prophet of the race, yearns. So Shelley says, of his poems in the 'Dedication of the Cenci,' 'They are dreams of what ought to be, or may be.'

What we *have* tried to do is to adduce evidence to show that he does arrive at his conclusions in a manner different from logical thought, seeing, instead of demonstrating; not different, however, in kind from our own conceptions in what we term 'daydream,' 'reveries,' 'musing,' 'vision,' 'ecstasy,' 'trance,' 'rapture,' or the like. For this kind of thinking we have no name, unless we use the term 'associative thought' as distinct from 'voluntary thought.' It is aroused by feeling, and it has no practical end; though, properly understood, it has a 'value' of its own. It can only come from a creative imagination. Men discount the dreamer as they discount their own dreams. They call him mad. He *is* mad, in a sense, as the lover is mad, who also makes his choice and arrives at conclusions, not by conscious argument, but by intuitions which, possibly, well up from the unconscious.[1] But his dreams, his visionary thoughts, are the source of all poetry, and make poets, as Shelley said, 'the hierophants of an unapprehended inspiration; the mirrors of the gigantic shadows futurity casts upon the present; the words which express what they understand not; the trumpets which sing to battle and feel not what they inspire; the influence which is moved not, but moves. Poets are the unacknowledged legislators of the world.'

Granted that the poet arrives at his ideas in this way, our next question must ask whether this way is valid.

---

[1] So Shakespeare:
'Lovers and madmen have such seething brains,
Such shaping fantasies, that apprehend
More than cool reason ever comprehends.
The lunatic, the lover, and the poet
Are of imagination all compact.'
Midsummer Night's Dream, Act V., sc. 1.

POET'S CONTRIBUTION TO IDEAS 25

Thus we arrive at the question we set out to answer, ' Is the poet's contribution to ideas valid ? '

Here again we desire to fall back on Aristotle's distinction between the ecstatic and euplastic poet. The latter's idea may or may not be valid. He may or may not be inspired. By conscious art he assumes an inspiration which is not his own. In a sense he is a copyist. A poet may be ecstatic in some poems, euplastic in others. In this chapter we use the word ' poet ' in the ecstatic sense.

How are we to show the validity of the ecstatic poet's ideas? Let us suppose that we are standing, on a clear day, on some mountain peak in Switzerland, and that before us stretches a glorious panorama of snow-covered mountains. Immediately, and intuitively, we know that the scene before us is beautiful. We do not need our guide to prove it to us. The scene strikes some inward faculty of appreciation of the beautiful, so that we *know* that, for us, it is beauty which we behold, though all the world should deny it. Furthermore, our experience fits in to other experiences in which we have gazed on natural beauty, and is one with them.

We believe that in a similar way there is such a thing as intuitive appreciation of truth, and intuitive acceptance of an idea as true. We *feel* it to be true, nor is there any more reason to believe that the idea is true because we feel it deeply, than that we feel it deeply just because it is true.[1] We do not wait for the logician or philosopher or theologian to give us their proofs and their authority. We are like the people described in our oldest Gospel, who were astonished at Christ's

---

[1] James Russell Lowell in ' Incidents in a Railroad Car ':
' All thought begins in feeling—wide
   In the great mass its base is hid,
   And, narrowing up to thought, stands glorified,
     A moveless pyramid.'
That is, the feeling is the foundation of the solid thought ; but we are not to say, ' We feel a thing deeply, therefore it is true,' but rather, ' It is true, therefore we feel it deeply.'

teaching; 'for He taught them as having authority, and not as the scribes.'[1] Yet the scribes were the very people who had external authority. But Christ's authority was the inward authority of truth, and its weight lay in the people's own intuitive appreciation of truth. He did not argue, but, when He spoke, something in the hearer leaped up in recognition of the truth.

The ecstatic poet 'sees,' and, if we read his poetry as poetry, he bears us up to the mountain-top so that we may share his experience, and then we see what he sees. We believe that when a poet writes in what we have called the 'ecstatic' sense, when his vision is not spoiled by personal opinion and prejudice, then he is able to discern truths to which, as yet, reason cannot attain, and, following him, we can discern them also. We do not learn; we discern.

And the difference is such as that between learning that spring has come because the calendar tells us so, and of going out on some sweet April morning, seeing for ourselves the flowers, hearing the birds, and feeling the vernal breezes on our brow. Then, with Wordsworth,

> We *see* into the life of things.

Yet this way which the poet has of *arriving* at his ideas is not to be thought less reasonable than the slower method of the logician. None of us would ever intuitively accept an idea as true unless in some way it harmonized with other ideas we had previously accepted as true; unless it could be built into the mental fabric erected with the material of a thousand previous experiences. When we have seen a mountain panorama and declared it beautiful, we may, if we like —though we rarely do it—examine the scene as to whether, and why, it fits in with other experiences

[1] Mark i. 22.

of the beautiful in nature. In the same way, when we have shared an experience with the poet, and intuitively felt his ideas to be valid, we may afterwards take their contents and ask if they harmonize with our mental world, and with human experience collected over as wide a field as possible. In a word, we may ask whether they make sense. These are the grounds on which an intuitive idea comes to be accepted as true.

But it is important to notice that to a less extent, but in precisely the same way, we do this also in the case of the scientist and the logician. Some of the hypotheses on which science stakes enormous issues are as yet a guess—the theory of electrons, for instance. We accept the guess, and then ask if it makes sense. The logician himself makes a guess, even in the syllogism; a guess that the mind is acting in a trustworthy manner, and not leading him into a subtle illusion, when he argues that if A equals B and B equals C, then A equals C. Is not our very satisfaction with what we call 'truth' in the nature of a guess? Truth, while we are human, and, indeed, until the whole universe is wound up, is a guess—the greatest degree of probability, the most satisfactory way of accounting for observed phenomena.

The method of the poet is different from that of the scientist or the logician, as we have shown; but for him the state of ecstasy is not abnormal, nor is it untrustworthy. It may be super-reasonable, but it is not more unreasonable than other more familiar processes of thought; and if the poet's contribution to ideas is not valid, neither is that of the scientist or the logician.

Yet this validity can only be affirmed of the ecstatic poet. He only is the true visionary, and therefore he it is who has given the best poetry to the world, provided that art has not hindered vision. With this provision we may say that in the best poetry we are nearest the sharing of the actual experience of the poet which gave birth to the poem. In the best poetry—from the poet's point of view—we most nearly see what he sees. The ideas in such poetry are those which have become his in vision, not as men gather their casual opinions. Therefore the ideas in the best poetry are more valid than those, say, of the euplastic poet. In other words, the worth of the poetry of a poem determines the value of its philosophic ideas ; for, although beauty and truth are not synonymous, in that they belong to different activities of the personality—emotion and intellection—yet their kinship is seen in the very fact that that personality is a unity. Keats would go farther, and say that beauty is truth, truth beauty. At any rate, ' whenever a fiction of the poetic mind wins us because of its beauty, we may be pretty sure that it embodies an idea which, if we could get it, would win our reasonable approval also. We can only feel the beauty of the fiction ; we can perhaps by analysis demonstrate the truth of the idea ; but our judgement is as much to be trusted in one case as in the other. We may indeed, by a transference of the terms, call the fiction " true," and speak of the truth of poetry. Keats, therefore, is essentially right when he says : " What the imagination seizes as beauty must be truth. . . ." Thus the poet dreams, and his dream seems idle, but when he awakes he finds there is a rational conception correspondent to it, and this is an addition to knowledge.'[1]

Thus we can accept Wordsworth's dictum that ' every poet is a teacher,' and respect his wish ' to be remembered as a teacher or as nothing ' ; for discernment is as legitimate a way of learning as is logic, and so much more pleasant that people in all ages and countries have gone to the poets and found them the greatest teachers of the human race. And this is true concerning religion.

A poem may treat of any subject ; for it is not the

[1] Prescott, *The Poetic Mind*, p. 84.

POET'S CONTRIBUTION TO IDEAS 29

subject, but the way in which it is treated, which constitutes the test as to whether it is good poetry or not. A poem may treat of a mathematical calculation, if that calculation has fired the poetic imagination with a new vision of the reign of law in the universe. A poem may have a loathsome subject as long as we are made to enjoy our loathing. A poem may contain argument—as 'Paradise Lost' does—as long as the poet can kindle it, and retain, in dealing with it, the poetic fire—as Milton does.

It is very important to our purpose to state that a poem is not *necessarily* less poetic when it treats of religious and philosophic ideas than when it treats of clouds and sunsets, so long as those ideas are treated poetically. It is not necessarily ruined if it has an *undertone* of moral significance, so long as it does not become predominantly didactic. In a matter like immortality, which we are to discuss, and by which we mean the conscious survival and indefinitely prolonged life of the human personality after death, the poet is going to help us more than the theologian. The latter, by his very training, is apt to be dogmatic, swayed by fears of being thought unorthodox, influenced by preconceived ideas and sometimes by ' convictions ' which have been handed down from bygone ages, but never dispassionately examined. The poet cares for none of these things :

> Contented if he might enjoy
> The things which others understand.[1]

Above all, he is not trying to prove an intellectual position. Concerning immortality there can be no ' proof.' The theologian himself can only speculate. Immortality is a conception to which reason has not yet climbed. Indeed, a rational view of life contains much to deny it. Only the poets have soared to that

[1] Wordsworth, ' A Poet's Epitaph.'

high altitude. It is their function to do this. Bacon, in *The Advancement of Learning*, says that the use of poetry ' hath been to give some shadow of satisfaction to the mind of man in those points wherein the nature of things doth deny it.' Who, then, can take us farther in our quest than the man who can both see and sing ? So let us turn to the poets,

>And hear the mighty stream of tendency
>Uttering, for elevation of our thought,
>A clear sonorous voice, inaudible
>To the vast multitude; whose doom it is
>To run the giddy round of vain delight,
>Or fret and labour on the Plain below.[1]

[1] Wordsworth, ' The Excursion,' Book ix.

II

THE DISCARDING OF ORTHODOX IDEAS OF IMMORTALITY

(Wordsworth and Shelley)

II
THE DISCARDING OF ORTHODOX IDEAS OF IMMORTALITY

I

WORDSWORTH (1770–1850)[1]

IN the mind of the poet there is a perpetual interplay between vision and opinion, and the one affects the other; but our quest is not so much that of the opinions of Wordsworth on the subject of the immortality of the soul. It is rather to catch the mood of the poet which drove him to write, and to see, as far as we can, what he saw, when, with the poet's vision, he contemplated the destinies of the human personality.

Yet the former is not irrelevant to our task. Room must be made for the fact that the vision of the poet is bound to be influenced by his private opinions. They will tend to colour his outlook. They must, therefore, be held in mind. These opinions will best be found in his letters, where we can without hesitation discern the opinions of Wordsworth himself.

In 1805, when his brother John, in command of the East Indiaman *Abergavenny*, was drowned, Wordsworth wrote as follows: ' Why have we sympathies that make the best of us so afraid of inflicting pain and sorrow which yet we see dealt about so lavishly by the Supreme Governor? Why should our notions of right towards each other, and to all sentient beings within our influence, differ so widely from what appears to be

---

[1] An article by the present writer on ' The Idea of Immortality in Wordsworth,' written as a preliminary study for this chapter, appeared in the *London Quarterly Review*, October 1924.

His notion and rule if everything were to end here?
Would it not be blasphemy to say that, upon the supposition of the thinking principle being destroyed by death, however inferior we may be to the great Cause and Ruler of things, we have more of love in our nature than He has? The thought is monstrous; and yet how to get rid of it, except upon the supposition of another and a better world, I do not see.' Again, in 1832, he wrote in regard to Coleridge: ' He and my beloved sister are now proceeding, as it were *pari passu*, along the path of sickness, I will not say towards the grave, but I trust towards a blessed immortality.' But the best evidence that Wordsworth had a strong belief in immortality is the beautiful story of the close of his life. His wife, on April 20, 1850, conveyed to Wordsworth the information that he was dying by saying, ' William, you are going to Dora' (their daughter, who died on July 10, 1847). The aged poet made no sign that he had even heard the words. ' More than twenty-four hours afterwards, one of his nieces came into the room, and was drawing aside the curtains of his chamber; and then, as if awakening from a quiet sleep, he said, " Is that Dora? "'[1]

We turn now to Wordsworth's poems, and ask, not only whether this belief is mirrored there, and is a mere acceptance of the orthodox creed of the day, but whether, as a poet, he makes any definite contribution to the form of belief in immortality; whether there is anything distinctive about it; whether that contribution has any value; and, if so, what it is.

Wordsworth reveals in a good many poems a belief in the orthodox theological view of his day, and in not a few he speaks of immortality without defining further what he means by it. We need not spend much time over these mere casual references to the subject, though it is relevant to take notice of them in our survey. Many of them, moreover, are passages of

[1] *William Wordsworth*, Harper, vol. ii., p. 436.

very great beauty. Take the one in 'The Excursion' (iv.) beginning:

> I cannot doubt that they whom you deplore
> Are glorified; or, if they sleep, shall wake
> From sleep, and dwell with God in endless love;

or the magnificent passage which closes Book v. of the same poem:

> Life is love and immortality,
> The being one, and one the element.
> There lies the channel and original bed,
> From the beginning, hollowed out and scooped
> For Man's affections—else betrayed and lost,
> And swallowed up 'mid deserts infinite.

'What is the death of Mr. Fox,' asks Wordsworth,

> more than this—
> That man, who is from God sent forth,
> Doth yet again to God return?
> Such ebb and flow must ever be,
> Then wherefore should we mourn?

Presumably the *locus classicus* in Wordsworth of the orthodox idea of immortality is the passage in Book xiv. of 'The Prelude.' The poet is speaking of spiritual love:

> This faculty hath been the feeding source
> Of our long labour: we have traced the stream
> From the blind cavern whence is faintly heard
> Its natal murmur; followed it to light
> And open day; accompanied its course
> Among the ways of Nature, for a time
> Lost sight of it bewildered and engulphed;
> Then given it greeting as it rose once more
> In strength, reflecting from its placid breast
> The works of man and face of human life;
> And lastly, from its progress have we drawn
> Faith in life endless, the sustaining thought
> Of human Being, Eternity, and God.

The Ecclesiastical Sonnet entitled 'Funeral Service' (xxxi.), and 'We are Seven,' seem to have been written for the specific purpose of expressing the idea of immortality as found in the creeds of the Church ; so also Sonnet xiv., where we find the lines :

> We know the arduous strife, the eternal laws
> To which the triumph of all good is given,
> High sacrifice, and labour without pause,
> Even to death : else wherefore should the eye
> Of man converse with immortality ?

In ' Epitaphs and Elegiac Pieces ' we naturally find references to the orthodox conception abounding ; but we pass on to discuss Wordsworth's more distinctive contributions to the idea we are studying. The well-known passage in ' The Prelude ' may perhaps be quoted in closing this section :

> Our destiny, our being's heart and home,
> Is with infinitude, and only there ;
> With hope it is, hope that can never die,
> Effort, and expectation, and desire,
> And something evermore about to be.

There is a suggestion in Wordsworth's poetry of what has been called the immortality of influence, an idea which is nowhere in English poetry so well expressed as in George Eliot's lines beginning :

> O may I join the choir invisible
> Of those immortal dead who live again
> In minds made better by their presence.

While Wordsworth has nothing so definitely Positivist as this, his lines at the close of the series of sonnets called ' The River Duddon ' are interesting in that they do suggest the idea that, while the human spirit may have no separate and conscious existence after death, yet the influence of a man's personality lives on in the lives of others, and passes on from them to those whom in their turn they influence. In this way a non-personal, corporate immortality can, in a mystical sense, be held. It should be said, however, that this is a theory consistent with that of a personal immortality. It is more important to say that the idea does not occur in Wordsworth with this possible exception, and that therefore it cannot be said to be a characteristic contribution of his mind to the theme of immortality.

It is enough to quote the words concerned:

Still glides the Stream, and shall for ever glide;
The Form remains, the Function never dies;
While we, the brave, the mighty, and the wise,
We Men, who in our morn of youth defied
The elements, must vanish—be it so!
Enough, if something from our hands have power
To live, and act, and serve the future hour;
And if, as toward the silent tomb we go,
Through love, through hope, and faith's transcendent dower,
We feel that we are greater than we know.

The view of immortality which most characterizes Wordsworth is that which is expounded in his famous 'Ode on the Intimations of Immortality from the Recollections of Early Childhood,' which was begun in 1802 and finished in 1806. Here we have a view expressed which is echoed in many other of Wordsworth's poems; and it is worth spending a little time on it, since, without an understanding of it, we find ourselves unable to understand a great deal of the poet's work. F. W. H. Myers calls it 'Wordsworth's most characteristic message'; and, though we may not agree with this superlative claim, the message is one of very great importance.

Over its origin we can be brief. It derives ultimately from Plato, where the doctrine of reminiscence is found more than once. Perhaps most fully it is found in *Phaedo* (72–3). There is little doubt, however, that Wordsworth did not get the idea from Plato, but from his friend Coleridge, from whose conversation he drank deep draughts of inspiration. In 1796, Coleridge received the news of the birth of his son, afterwards called

Hartley, and on this event Coleridge wrote as follows:

> Oft o'er my brain does that strong fancy roll
> Which makes the present (while the flash doth last)
> Seem a mere semblance of some unknown past,
> Mixed with such feelings, as perplex the soul
> Self-questioned in her sleep; and some have said
> We lived, ere yet this robe of flesh we wore.

In a note appended to this sonnet, Coleridge acknowledges his indebtedness to Plato's *Phaedo*. When we find in the ' Immortality Ode ' of 1802 the line

> A six years Darling of a pigmy size,

and note also that Wordsworth's poem ' To H. C., Six Years Old,' also bears the date 1802, it does not seem unlikely that the birth of Hartley Coleridge led first to the poem, based on Plato, which Coleridge wrote, and that then Wordsworth either saw the poem, or the two friends had a conversation on the whole issue raised, or possibly both, and that Wordsworth, having let his thoughts simmer, as we know he was fond of doing before he committed them to writing, began six years later, both the ' Immortality Ode ' and the poem ' To H. C.'[1]

Weight is lent to the suggestion I have made that the two friends had a conversation about the matter, or perhaps many conversations, by the fact that Wordsworth did not finish the ' Immortality Ode ' until 1806; and in 1805 he seems to have stuck fast in the middle of it, for he wrote to Beaumont, ' Should Coleridge return, so that I might have some conversation with him, I should go on swimmingly.' So much for the origin of the great ode.

What was the theory to which Wordsworth gives expression in it? It is important to realize, in the first

---

[1] Garrod accepts this conclusion, but points out that the verses ' To H. C., Six Years Old,' were quoted by Coleridge in ' Anima Poetae,' dated 1801, when Hartley was only four years old, and that the first edition of the great ode has
' A four years Darling of a pigmy size.'
He suggests that the necessary alterations were made because the figure six represents better the age of a child such as the poet describes.

place, that, wherever he got it, it is leagues removed from Plato's doctrine of reminiscence,[1] which is an attempt to explain why we appear to know certain facts without ever having learned them (cf. *Phaedo*, 72, and *The Meno*, 82). It is suggested that we remember on earth ideas which we must have brought with us from some pre-natal existence. To Plato, the world of ideas alone has truth. The senses are sources of error. We should escape as far as possible from their contamination. We come to the truth of things by getting away from eyes and ears. Wordsworth's theory, on the other hand, has been called a 'romance of sensation.' He adapts an idea designed by Plato to explain how we arrive at certain conclusions amid the illusions of the senses, in order to show that the reality of the eternal is evidenced *by* the senses. To Wordsworth, truth comes through sense-perception. The voice of a cuckoo, the sight of a rainbow—poems concerning which, it is interesting to note, were commenced the same week as the 'Immortality Ode'—these are the things which produce in the poet a link with an unseen world of reality which long ago, before birth, he knew, and in which his spirit revelled. In childhood he is nearer to that pre-natal life, and therefore, to the child, gleams from that wondrous world are far more numerous and vivid than to the adult. As he grows up he gets farther and farther away from that life, and the gleams become rarer and fainter.

> There was a time when meadow, grove and stream,
> The earth, and every common light,
>   To me did seem
> Apparelled in celestial light,
> The glory and the freshness of a dream.
> It is not now as it hath been of yore :—
>   Turn whereso'er I may,
>   By night or day,
> The things which I have seen I now can see no more.

[1] This point is admirably worked out in *Wordsworth*, H. W. Garrod, p. 115 et seq.

40 THE AFTER-WORLD OF THE POETS

The child, in Wordsworth's view, is, as Tennyson said later, ' new to earth and sky,' but he discerns in the universe its kinship with that spiritual world from which he has come, and sees manifested in terms of material beauty here on earth that which reminds him of what he realized in terms of spiritual beauty in the former life.

> Our birth is but a sleep and a forgetting:
> The Soul that rises with us, our life's Star,
>   Hath had elsewhere its setting,
>   And cometh from afar:
> Not in entire forgetfulness,
> And not in utter nakedness,
> But trailing clouds of glory do we come
> From God, who is our home:
> Heaven lies about us in our infancy!

There is another difference worth noting between Wordsworth's conception and Plato's, a difference that takes Wordsworth farther even than Plato from the orthodox Christian position. Wordsworth draws the conclusions that the child is nearer heaven than the man, and that flashes of recollection of the beauties of the eternal world become rarer, and that thus the child is the best philosopher.

> Shades of the prison-house begin to close
>   Upon the growing Boy.

But the light becomes dimmer and dimmer.

> At length the Man perceives it die away,
> And fade into the light of common day.

Plato, on the contrary, makes the grown man the better philosopher, and more receptive to beauty and truth than the child.

There are interesting indications that Wordsworth in later life had some qualms about the theory. Perhaps they were started by Coleridge, who in *Biographia*

Literaria warns the reader against taking Wordsworth's doctrine of pre-existence in any literal sense. Coleridge, it is said, did not take it seriously, and did not believe that Plato believed the doctrine of reminiscence. If Wordsworth were merely toying with a fancy in this 'Immortality Ode,' we should be inclined to think that he did not seriously accept its truth and validity. But possibly, as we shall see, the qualms referred to were occasioned by the knowledge that his views were scarcely in harmony with orthodox theology. More probably, on the other hand, the famous ode is the result of what we called, in the first chapter, 'visionary thought,' and the qualifications added later are the result of sober reasoning. The ode is the work of the inspired poet. The modifications are in the nature of a compromising safeguard against criticism.

Whether Wordsworth himself accepted the conception included in the 'Immortality Ode' is an important question. Our answer will depend, in the first place, on whether the conception is embodied in other poems also, and, in the second place, whether there is anything in his later poems or letters which would lead us to believe that he ever denied its truth.

The idea of the 'Immortality Ode' emerges first in the lines beginning:

> My heart leaps up when I behold
> A rainbow in the sky.

The last lines of this little poem are prefixed to the 1815 edition of the great ode:

> The Child is father of the Man;
> And I could wish my days to be
> Bound each to each by natural piety.

We naturally look for the same idea in his poem 'To the Cuckoo,' since we know, from entries in Dorothy Wordsworth's Journal, that the poet was busy with it

42 THE AFTER-WORLD OF THE POETS

at the same time. Nor are we disappointed. The cuckoo's voice brings to him

> a tale
> Of visionary hours,

and of the days of boyhood, helping him to

> beget
> That golden time again.

And in the last verse we are reminded of the words of Wordsworth quoted in the Fenwick note in the great ode : ' Many times while going to school have I grasped a wall or tree to recall myself from this abyss of idealism to the reality.'

> O blessed Bird! the earth we pace
> Again appears to be
> An unsubstantial, faery place ;
> That is fit home for Thee !

In the last verse of the ' Anecdote for Fathers,' in the sonnet beginning ' It is a beauteous evening, calm and free,' where Wordsworth says of his French daughter, Caroline, that she lies ' in Abraham's bosom all the year,' we find the same thought. We are told of the ' Happy Warrior ' that he

> hath wrought
> Upon the plan that pleased his boyish thought :

and in the ode ' composed upon an evening of extraordinary splendour and beauty ' (1818) we find a pathetic reference to the light which, in the ' Immortality Ode,' is called the ' fountain light of all our day ' and the ' master light of all our seeing ' :

> Oh, let thy grace remind me of the light
> Full early lost, and fruitlessly deplored ;
> Which, at this moment, on my waking sight
> Appears to shine, by miracle restored ;

> My soul, though yet confined to earth,
> Rejoices in a second birth!
> —'Tis past; the visionary splendour fades;
> And night approaches with her shade.

And in a magnificent passage in 'The Prelude' (Book xii.) the same idea emerges:

> Oh! mystery of man, from what a depth
> Proceed thy honours. I am lost, but see
> In simple childhood something of the base
> On which thy greatness stands; but this I feel,
> That from thyself it comes, that thou must give,
> Else never can receive. The days gone by
> Return upon me almost from the dawn
> Of life; the hiding-places of man's power
> Open; I would approach them, but they close.
> I see by glimpses now; when age comes on,
> May scarcely see at all.

It can scarcely be claimed that Wordsworth was toying temporarily with an idea when we find references to it so widely diffused throughout his work as the above quotations show it to be. It may fairly be claimed that Wordsworth held that the little child born into the world came from an immortal sphere of beauty and love, and that the highest and noblest moments of manhood, the clearest conceptions, the purest and most unselfish deeds, become possible when flashes of the once native glory pierced through the mists of the accumulated years of life in this far grosser world.

Does Wordsworth ever contradict the idea? 'I think it right,' he says in a Fenwick note, ' to protest against a conclusion, which has given pain to some good and pious persons, that I meant to inculcate such a belief. It is far too shadowy a notion to be recommended to faith as more than an element in our instincts of immortality. But let us bear in mind that, though the idea is not advanced in revelation, there is nothing there to contradict it, and the fall of man presents an analogy in its favour.'

One is inclined to the belief that the note is an attempt of the later Wordsworth, confessedly less of a poet than before, to defend the ideas in the poetic vision which inspired the great ode, and to endeavour to make them harmonize with the orthodox teaching of the Church. When we consider how often in Wordsworth the idea is repeated, and that it is never denied, we are justified in regarding it as a tenet of his poetic faith.

In seeking to appraise its value, we may note some arguments against it. We must admit that it would be impossible to prove that the child may not have brought into this world memories of a supposed brighter and fairer one. It may be that in certain directions a child has a clearer perception of things as they are than has the adult. But the possibility, even if true, seems of little value, since the child cannot adequately express himself when the perceptions are most clear; is only reminded of

> That imperial Palace whence he came

by detecting the immanence of its same pervading spirit in nature; and that these memories become more and more indistinct and blurred as time goes on. The thought, from one point of view seems rather depressing; for loss of light cannot find adequate compensation in the mere memory of more illumined days, or in the hope that in ten thousand years[1] the soul may regain that imperial palace.

Moreover, there are facts about childhood which would seem to contradict the idea. In the poem to his infant daughter, Wordsworth speaks of her

> sinless progress, through a world
> By sorrows darkened and by care disturbed,
> Apt likeness bears to hers, through gathered clouds,
> Moving untouched in silver purity,
> And cheering oft-times their reluctant gloom.
> Fair are ye both, and both are free from stain.

[1] Plato's figure.

This is a departure from the orthodox theological belief in the doctrine of original sin, in favour of Rousseau's doctrine of original goodness, which, of course, matters nothing. But does it explain the facts? Though we may break from the too rigid emphasis which the doctrine of original sin has received in the past, is it not more true to the perceived facts of childhood than the idea in the ' Immortality Ode ' and elsewhere? Do we not find ourselves in the world with a definite bias towards the choice of evil rather than good, and, if this be true, shall we not have to look in other directions for an explanation of the phenomenon Wordsworth's theory attempts to explain?

With psychological research we cannot concern ourselves here ; but we may note that it has been established that under certain conditions of hypnosis a man can remember events that happened as early as the first years of life, but under no conditions yet discovered can go back farther, and that none of the brilliant experiments conducted by Professor William Brown[1] lend any support to the Wordsworthian hypothesis.

The gravest criticism of the idea, however, from the point of view of the student of immortality, is that it has nothing to do with immortality in the sense in which that term is usually understood and applied. We have defined immortality as the conscious survival, and indefinitely prolonged existence of the human personality after death ; and, though one might widen the definition and look before as well as after, it is with the future that we are concerned here. The modern thinker, with a different explanation of the phenomena which caused Plato to frame his doctrine of reminiscence, pays little heed to the speculative possibility of pre-existence, and feels that, even if accepted, it supplies little evidence for immortality as we have defined it, for the idea of pre-existence not defined as

[1] Quoted in *King's College Lectures on Immortality*, p. 125 et seq.

personal is no evidence for a post-existence which is personal.

Wordsworth sets before us an ideal of so binding our days together 'by natural piety' that the light of infancy may be retained to illumine old age and kindle a hope of life after death. This the 'Happy Warrior' is conceived as doing. But, by the poet's own theory, that light melts into the light of common day, and becomes at last a memory. He imagines that memory powerful enough to achieve the end he desires:

> What though the radiance which was once so bright
> Be now *for ever* taken from my sight,
> Though nothing can bring back the hour
> Of splendour in the grass, of glory in the flower;
> We will grieve not, rather find
> Strength in what remains behind;
> In the primal sympathy
> Which having been must ever be;
> In the soothing thoughts that spring
> Out of human suffering;
> In the faith that looks through death,
> In years that bring the philosophic mind.

We wonder whether in practice the memory is powerful enough to do this. Such a feat of memory would indeed be 'emotion recollected in tranquillity'; but is not the poet deluding himself that he is still in some kind of contact—though undetected—with the world of eternal beauty which he saw in childhood's years? The falling off in Wordsworth's own poetry would seem to answer this question.

On the other hand, there are considerations which make Wordsworth's idea very attractive. Pre-existence is not an unreasonable speculation.[1] It is as reasonable a hypothesis as to the manner in which we become possessed of a soul as is that of creationism—that the soul of the child is created anew at conception.

[1] It was tenaciously held by Origen, *c.* 185–254.

Moreover, there *is* something about a sunset,[1] about even

> the meanest flower that blows,

which claims kinship with something within ourselves. It is as though a photograph of his mother were thrust before the eyes of a man who had wandered away from home. Natural beauty does seem to remind us that

> we come
> From God, who is our home.

That beauty makes us sad. Our very sadness seems to point forward, as well as backward, to a time when the soul will revel in the fullness of life from which the flesh restrains it here on earth; when it will gaze upon the beauty of which natural beauty is but a shadow.

Again, the time of youth is certainly the time when such experiences are most common, at least for most men; not necessarily, however, because they lose the faculty of reason, but because associative thought or dreaming is, as we grow older, banished by the constant need for conscious and directed thought. Yet in the silences that sometimes fall on the soul the old sensations recur:

> in a season of calm weather
> Though inland far we be,
> Our souls have sight of that immortal sea
> Which brought us hither,
> Can in a moment travel thither,
> And see the Children sport upon the shore,
> And hear the mighty waters rolling evermore.

It is at any rate the poetic faith of Wordsworth that in infancy we have direct vision of the eternal world; that gradually this vision fades, but that again and again memories of that world are awakened by natural

---

[1] ' Ne'er can I believe
That this magnificence is wholly thine;
From worlds not quickened by the Sun
A portion of the gift is won.'

beauty ; and sometimes vision, for a brief and fleeting moment, is restored. All this convinces us that we belong to a spiritual order, and

> though nothing can bring back the hour
> Of splendour in the grass, of glory in the flower ;
> We will grieve not, rather find
> Strength . . .
> In the faith that looks through death,
> In years that bring the philosophic mind.

An idea which a seer like Wordsworth crystallizes into such magic words as those of the great ode is one to be held in the mind with reverence and regard.

Wordsworth, so it seems to us, strikes out an avenue by which we approach the poetic thought of the nineteenth century on the subject of immortality. It is significant to note the source to which he turns. He turns to Platonism, and, though he modifies it by Christianity, he never turns to the New Testament for any assurance on the subject. The road which Wordsworth opened marks a departure from orthodox religious thought. And down that road other poets of the century followed.

2

SHELLEY (1792–1822)

It will seem strange to some that we should look for the development of an idea which is partly religious in the work of a man who called himself an atheist. Yet the attitude of Shelley towards this question is most important. His break with orthodoxy was the best thing that could happen to the theology of his day. In order that the importance of Shelley to religious thought may be estimated, it will be worth while to consider the poet's mentality.

We think it would be too much to say that Shelley was a religious man. A religious man recognizes a bond between himself and God, or the gods, which involves some measure of obedience. Shelley was, however, a man of fine moral fibre, an ecstatic poet, and one who loved justice, liberty, and truth with all the passion of his soul. Nor did he close his mind to the alleged truths of religion, but, on the contrary, was intensely interested in them. Something must be said to substantiate this last sentence.

'As I call Shelley a moral man,' says Browning, in his admirable *Essay on Shelley*, ' because he was true, simple-hearted, and brave, and because what he acted corresponded to what he knew, so I called him a man of religious mind, because every audacious negative cast up by him against the divine was interpenetrated with a mood of reverence and adoration, and because I find him everywhere taking for granted some of the capital dogmas of Christianity while most vehemently denying their historical basement.'[1]

Again, those who are ready to dub Shelley as no more than a libertine may well ponder the fact that not many youths of twenty-one, even though they be deemed religious, have read the Bible through four times, as Shelley had by 1813. We find him, on August 18, 1812, writing thus to Mr. Thomas Hookham: ' I shall, if possible, prepare a volume of essays, moral and religious, by November.' On December 17 he writes again to Hookham enclosing a MS. entitled *Biblical Extracts*, which, however, was never published. It was probably an attempt to outline the teaching of Jesus in its essential features without the addition of the miraculous and without theological accretions.

At one period it seems that Shelley had thoughts of entering the ministry. When, in 1815, he was walking with his friend, Peacock, in a country village, he saw a vicarage nestling among the trees, and his mind turned towards the career of a minister. With characteristic impulsiveness, he said, ' I feel strongly inclined to enter the Church. . . . Of the moral doctrines

[1] Browning, *An Essay on Shelley* (Blackwell), p. 79.

of Christianity I am a more decided disciple than many of its more ostentatious professors.' And consider how much good a good clergyman may do.' Dowden comments that some Anglican bishop was mercifully delivered from the Rev. Percy B. Shelley.[1] The present writer is inclined to the opposite view. Who knows that Shelley might not have stirred the Church up to re-think her position, re-word her creeds, put away her hypocrisy, and deliver the nation from spiritual sleeping sickness?

An important point to notice, in order to appreciate Shelley's attitude to religion, is that he would not accept a dogma, and believe it, merely because it was generally believed and taught in the creeds. If his friends suggested that many people held the creeds to be true, but applied to their language a private interpretation, knowing that their statement would be taken in an entirely different sense, or made concerning them mental reservations, Shelley's crystal-clear mind saw through the device at once, and he called it by its true name, insincerity, and often hypocrisy; at best, intellectual cowardice. He refused to hold that an 'infallibility,' overthrown by even a moment's thoughtful inquiry, can be accepted on the ground of utility by an intelligent and self-respecting person. If his enemies thundered their anathemas at him for heresy and tried to frighten him with all the horrors of their vulgar hell, he grew the more convinced that a ' truth ' which needed such support must be partly, if not wholly, false. His whole soul, free as the winds, rebelled against the pitiful mentality which, for so many bleak and dreary centuries, has imagined that persecution is an adequate answer to argument.

All this no doubt hurt his friends and goaded his enemies. Such transparent honesty of mind hurts people, because people hate to be made to think. Shelley made them think. It undoubtedly requires

---

[1] Dowden, *Life of Shelley*, vol. i., p. 512.

courage to take a tenet of one's faith, which one may have held for half a century, and ask two questions about it; first, ' What does it mean ? ' and second, ' Is it true ? ' The intellectual honesty of Shelley demanded that both questions should be asked and answered, and, if a doctrine were found untenable, he broke it, however venerable it might be.

The moral character of Shelley has, of course, often been discussed, and we need not take much time with it here. Let us briefly consider a few facts. In tracing his life-story we are watching one who, as a boy of ten, would rather be flogged than laugh at the unsavoury jests of the head master at Sion House, Isleworth, his first school,[1] who as a youth at Oxford cannot pass a peasant girl at the roadside who looked starved and cold, but must needs get warm milk and give it her; who, later, will take no sugar in his tea because the produce of the cane was obtained by slave labour; who, when he was financially embarrassed, gave two pounds to a fund raised on behalf of the relatives of some riotous framebreakers executed at York in 1813, twenty pounds to John and Leigh Hunt, who were fined a thousand pounds—unjustly, as Shelley thought —for outspoken political articles in the *Examiner*, and a large sum—his wife says five hundred pounds—in relief of peasants at Tanyralt, Carnarvonshire, who suffered in attempting to reclaim, under the direction of a certain Mr. Madocks, a large tract of land from the insatiable maw of the sea.

It would be foolish to try to whitewash Shelley's character by arraying a number of his kindly deeds. There is, we think, no doubt that his treatment of his wife Harriet was unethical. Sometimes he shows an amazing ignorance of women, as when, eloping with Mary, he writes inviting Harriet to join them, and is

---

[1] Shelley hated obscenity, which in his *Defence of Poetry* he defines as blasphemy against the divine beauty of life. Mary Shelley tells how Pacchiani, an Italian dentist, ' disgusted Shelley by telling a dirty story.'

aggrieved at her refusal. But the facts have not always been looked at from Shelley's point of view. Let us briefly attempt this. Granted that he imagines at the age of nineteen that he loves a schoolgirl of sixteen called Harriet Westbrook, that he elopes with her and marries her at Edinburgh in 1811; yet let it also be remembered that before he married her he had promised that, if she were in trouble and needed him, he would come to her assistance, and that she piteously appealed to him for help. And Shelley could never refuse help to any one who was in trouble, let alone a girl in tears. It should also be remembered that before his marriage he stated quite definitely that he did not regard any marriage tie as binding save that of love, and that, if either ceased to love, then freedom from the bond must be allowed. He tells us, in 'Epipsychidion':

> I never was attached to that great sect,
> Whose doctrine is, that each one should select
> Out of the crowd a mistress or a friend,
> And all the rest, though fair and wise, commend
> To cold oblivion, though it is the code
> Of modern morals, and the beaten road
> Which those poor slaves with weary footsteps tread,
> Who travel to their home among the dead
> By the broad highway of the world, and so
> With one chained friend, perhaps a jealous foe,
> The dreariest and the longest journey go.

We ought not to forget that Harriet, as well as Shelley, altered. She grew worldly, demanding a carriage, and new dresses beyond the possibilities of Shelley's pocket and totally opposed to his tastes. She was no longer Shelley's admiring disciple. She preferred the advice of her older sister Eliza, who lived with them, and who was a constant thorn in Shelley's side.

Yet when Harriet left him he constantly asked her to

return. We note in this connexion the sonnet, 'To Harriet, May 1814,' beginning,

> Thy look of love has power to calm
> The stormiest passions of my soul;

and ending,

> O deign a nobler pride to prove,
> And pity if thou canst not love.

When all that he could do was unavailing to bring Harriet back, he made her a handsome allowance. To be fair to Shelley, we ought not to omit to mention that when, after her suicide, the unfortunate Harriet's body was dragged from the Serpentine, the fact was made public that had she lived a little longer she would have borne a child, the father of which could not have been Shelley. We are not trying to take all blame from Shelley and fasten it on Harriet, but the reverse process has been the method of some literary critics. It is better to note the facts, and refrain from allotting blame at all, but disabusing the mind of the notion that Shelley's thoughts rose from so perverse and immoral a mentality as to be hardly worth considering in relation to a religious idea.[1]

Shelley's love for Mary Godwin led him to break the conventions of society; but here, again, his action in carrying her off was not out of harmony with his philosophy, which he had learned mainly from her father. His poem 'To Mary Wollstonecraft Godwin' beginning:

> Mine eyes were dim with tears unshed,

speaks of the anguish of spirit which had become his through the terrible events connected with the break with Harriet.

---

[1] Kingsley compared the habit of reading Shelley to that of secretly drinking eau-de-Cologne. Matthew Arnold speaks of Shelley's 'unwholesome and seductive atmosphere.' Hazlitt said that 'no one was ever wiser or better for reading Shelley'; and even the gentle Lamb said Shelley's poems were 'thin sown with profit.'

Mary Shelley assures us that, were all the facts known, Shelley would be exonerated from blame; and no one has produced evidence which carries the opposite conclusion in any convincing way. Shelley himself, writing to Southey in reply to the latter's cruel article in the *Quarterly Review*, says: ' I am innocent of ill, either done or intended; the consequences you allude to flowed in no respect from me. If you were my friend, I could tell you a history which would make you open your eyes; but I shall certainly never make the public my familiar confidant ' And, whatever our private estimate of Shelley's character may be, we cannot doubt his sincerity. ' Whatever Shelley was,' says Browning,[1] ' he was with an admirable sincerity.'

The world will never be able to forget, apparently, that Shelley called himself an atheist; and it will continue to use his own word against him for all time. There were three occasions when Shelley pronounced himself an atheist. It is important, before we discuss his contribution to a semi-religious problem, that we should examine and inquire into their significance.

The first occasion was the publication, in February 1811, while Shelley was a youth of nineteen at Oxford, of a pamphlet entitled *The Necessity of Atheism*. We do not propose to examine it in detail. Commencing with the premiss that the senses are the sole source of knowledge, Shelley points out that no proof of the existence of God can be maintained in that direction. He sets aside the evidence of reason, claiming that the eternal existence of matter is more reasonable than that it had a beginning in time and that it therefore had a cause. The testimony of men Shelley rejects, since men ask us to believe something which is contra-rational; not miracles only, but a God who, they say, *commanded* that men should believe in Him, whereas belief is not volitional. We cannot believe anything

[1] *An Essay on Shelley.* p. 75.

or in any one merely because we are commanded to do so.

It is not relevant to our subject to discuss the pamphlet, which was a symptom of the growing-pains of a soul in quest of truth, and which was the impulsive fruit of a phase of experience through which every one passes who strives to think his way through the great questions of religion, and which has something of the element of a practical joke at the bottom of it.

That which is most noteworthy about it from our point of view, since it gives us insight into the poet's mind, is the 'Advertisement,' or Foreword, which runs as follows: 'As a love of truth is the only motive which actuates the author of this little tract, he earnestly entreats that those of his readers who may discover any deficiency in his reasoning, or may be in possession of proofs which his mind could never obtain, would offer them, together with their objections, to the Public, as briefly, as methodically, as plainly, as he has taken the liberty of doing. THROUGH DEFICIENCY OF PROOF[1]—AN ATHEIST.'

Shelley, because he would not deny authorship, was expelled immediately from Oxford and branded with the epithet atheist. He left the day after publication. The iron entered his soul. Bitterly he accepted the title, and came at length to regard it as a kind of banner under which to fight the battle for liberty of thought, for re-statement, and for inquiry against those whose only weapons were persecution and abuse.

The second occasion on which Shelley styled himself an atheist was an entry he made in the 'Travellers' Album' at Montanvert, in Switzerland. The glories of nature had uplifted and charmed his spirit. When he came to sign the book at the hotel where he stayed, he noticed with undisguised contempt the conventional religious phrases which preceded most of the signatures. In a mood of pique, he determined that, on the one

[1] Printed in capitals in the original.

hand, he would break away from what he deemed hypocrisy manifested in the pious phrases of other visitors, and, on the other hand, that he would not be swept into allegiance to any form of doctrinal belief by the emotion kindled by the glorious scenery about him. Thus he wrote in Greek the words, ' I am a philanthropist, a democrat, and an atheist,'[1] and then signed his name. Again his impish and mischievous mood interprets his act.

The third occasion on which he definitely accepted the title is related by Trelawney. In 1822, the year of Shelley's death, Trelawney asked him, ' Why do you call yourself an atheist ? It annihilates you in this world.' ' It is a good word of abuse to stop discussion,' said Shelley, ' a painted devil to frighten the foolish, a threat to intimidate the wise and good. I use it to express my abhorrence of superstition. I took up the word as a knight takes up a gauntlet in defiance of injustice.'

If this be clearly understood—that his atheism, so called, was not a denial of God, but a denial of the kind of God the current theology supposed, and that his acceptance of the epithet ' atheist ' was the acceptance of a challenge to enter a great battle—then we may follow him into various campaigns and watch him fighting, his soul on fire for justice ; or, if it be preferred, a soul possessed of two great hatreds, a hatred of insincerity and anything approaching a lie, however venerable ; and a hatred of cruelty and injustice. And these principles, which actuated all Shelley's thought and conduct, make relevant to him words which Lord Morley spoke of Gladstone when he said that ' active hatred of cruelty, injustice, and oppression is perhaps the main difference between a good man and a bad one.'[2]

[1] $\epsilon\dot{\iota}\mu\iota\ \phi\iota\lambda\acute{a}\nu\theta\rho\omega\pi\sigma s\ \delta\eta\mu\omicron\kappa\rho\alpha\tau\iota\kappa\sigma s\ \tau\iota\ \ddot{a}\theta\epsilon\sigma s\ \tau\epsilon$. A later comer, it is said, added the word $\mu\omega\rho\sigma s$ (fool), and Byron, visiting Montanvert subsequently, effaced both $\ddot{a}\theta\epsilon\sigma s$ and $\mu\omega\rho\sigma s$.
[2] *Life of Gladstone*, vol. i., p. 196.

'To Shelley,' writes Mary, his wife, 'the rights of intellect were sacred, and all kings, teachers, or priests who sought to circumscribe the activity of discussion, and check by force the full development of the reasoning powers, he regarded as enemies to the independence of man. . . . He regarded conventional religion as gross, contradictory, and tending to oppression and cruelty. . . . He saw, moreover, that the Christianity of worldly-minded men is not sincere, that their practice is at war with their profession.'

We have taken up a good deal of space in discussing Shelley's mentality, because it seemed necessary to clear away the misconception, once held tenaciously, that he was an ordinary libertine and atheist. If it were relevant, it would be interesting to notice that the poet deals with such subjects as the Atonement, the Virgin Birth, the Inspiration of the Bible, the Character of God, and the Person of Christ—subjects in which he would not even be interested if he had been all he has sometimes been represented as being. In every subject he shows the same attitude. There is a fierce intellectual honesty, a refusal to accept any position merely because it is orthodox or venerable. There is a passion to investigate, to inquire, to examine, and to harmonize all theological positions with the conception of God as wise, just, and loving. When we turn to the idea of the possible life of the soul after death we find the same attitude. We believe it has never yet been recognized how important is Shelley's contribution to ideas on this subject. We believe that he was one of the first and the most powerful of prophets to refuse to accept the dismal doctrines of hell, and to set afoot the spirit of theological inquiry and revolt which untrammelled the religious thinking of the nineteenth century alike in theology, in literature and in art. We go so far as to say, indeed, what we have never seen suggested before—that the notions of hell which orthodoxy then promulgated affected him so deeply as to become an obsession. They offended his extreme sensitiveness. They outraged both the ideas which were the governing ideas of his whole life—justice and truth. We believe that his reaction against them explains how a man, keenly interested in religious thought, came to hate violently all its organized forms and its official representatives.

Shelley had what the newer psychologists would call a ' complex ' on the subject of hell. Of all the religious subjects mentioned, reference is most often made to this. We have made an attempt to count in his complete works, both prose and poetry, all the subjects directly related to religion. Of all mention of these subjects, over fifty per cent. are definite references to hell and over twenty-five per cent. are definite references to the life after death, without specific description of happiness or suffering. We thus see that, of all the religious subjects Shelley mentioned, the life after death has an importance indicated by the fact that it is mentioned seventy-five times out of every hundred of any mention of religious subjects whatever. In view of the conclusions which we think must be drawn from this consideration, it will be necessary to quote a number of them, the more so that we have never seen this point made before ; and yet it does seem important in order to arrive at an understanding of Shelley's contribution to theological and philosophical thought. The order of the quotations has been determined by that in which the various works were published.

It is surely indicative of much that when, as a little boy playing about the grounds of Field Place, near Horsham, Sussex, where he was born, Shelley set fire to a stack of faggots, his excuse was that he wanted ' a little hell of his own.' Few children, we are bound to think, would use such an expression, since it is to be hoped that few children, even in those days, would have been given the revolting conceptions of punishment after death which disfigured the theology of the time, and which had evidently, and most unfortunately been allowed to sear and stain the child-mind of the future poet.

Turning to his earliest work, 'Zastrozzi,' we find at once a tyrant and a victim, typical actors in all Shelleyan phantasmagoria. The execrable Zastrozzi says to his friend, concerning the fate of the victim Verezzi, ' Ugo, he shall die—die by the most hellish torments. I give myself up to fate : I will taste revenge ; for revenge is sweeter than life ; and even were I to die with him, and, as the punishment of my crime, *be instantly plunged into eternal torments*, I should taste superior joy in recollecting the sweet moment of his destruction. *O would that destruction could be eternal.*'[1] And in the same work : ' The guilty Matilda shrunk at death . . . her soul had caught a glimpse of the misery which awaits the wicked hereafter.'[2]

When we turn to ' St. Irvyne, or The Rosicrucian,' we see Wolfstein contemplating suicide by throwing himself over an Alpine precipice, and thus soliloquizing: 'Into this, then, shall I plunge myself ? . . . and by one rash act endanger perhaps eternal happiness— deliver myself up perhaps to the anticipation and experience of never-ending *torments*.'[3] Later he again contemplates the fact that, though ' now exulting in youthful health and vigour, the time would come, the dreadful day of retribution, when endless damnation would yawn beneath his feet and he would shrink from *eternal punishment*.' And, again : ' I may suffer, for this premeditated act, tortures now inconceivable. I may writhe, convulsed in immaterial agony, for ever and ever.' Eloise is supposed to find comfort in the thought that her enemy will ' howl with the fiends of darkness in never-ending misery,'[4] and the book closes

[1] *Prose Works*, ed. Forman, vol. i., p. 17.
[2] Ibid., vol. i., p. 138.
[3] Ibid., vol. i., p. 165.
[4] Ibid., vol. i., p. 264.

with Ginotti doomed to 'a dateless and hopeless eternity of horror.'[1]

In *The Necessity of Atheism*, Shelley, as we have noted in an earlier connexion, scorns a God who *commands* belief and proposes ' the highest rewards for faith, eternal punishment for disbelief.'

> There needeth not the hell that bigots frame
> To punish those who err,

Shelley tells us in ' Queen Mab ' (begun in 1810 and finished in 1813), and in the same poem he breaks out passionately against the three words which he says tyrants use—God, hell, and heaven.

> A vengeful, pitiless, and almighty fiend,
> Whose mercy is a nickname for the rage
> Of tameless tigers hungering for blood.
> Hell, a red gulph of everlasting fire,
> Where poisonous and undying worms prolong
> Eternal misery to those hapless slaves
> Whose life has been a penance for its crimes.
> And Heaven, a meed for those who dare belie
> Their human nature, quake, believe, and cringe
> Before the mockeries of earthly power.

And again :

> The self-sufficing, the omnipotent,
> The merciful, and the avenging God !
> Who, prototype of human misrule, sits
> High in Heaven's realm, upon a golden throne,
> Even like an earthly king ; and whose dread work,
> Hell, gapes for ever for the unhappy slaves
> Of fate, whom he created, in his sport,
> To triumph in their torments when they fell !

In a ' Refutation of Deism ' (1814) Shelley pursues the same theme, and condemns God for sentencing souls to hell for being what He made them.[2]

In his *Essay on Christianity* (1816), Shelley argues strongly against the current conceptions of hell.

[1] *Prose Works*, vol. i., p. 298.
[2] Ibid., vol. ii., p. 44.

' Jesus Christ would hardly have cited, as an example of all that is gentle and beneficent and compassionate, a Being who shall deliberately scheme to inflict on a large portion of the human race tortures indescribably intense and indefinitely protracted ; who shall inflict them, too, without any mistake as to the true nature of pain—without any view to future good—merely because it is just. . . . It is not to be believed that hell or punishment was the conception of this daring mind. It is not to be believed that the most prominent group of this picture, which is framed so heart-moving and lovely—the accomplishment of all human hope, the extinction of all morbid fear and anguish—would consist of millions of sensitive beings enduring, in every variety of torture which Omniscient vengeance could invent, immortal agony. Jesus Christ opposed with earnest eloquence the panic fears and hateful superstitions which have enslaved mankind for ages. . . . It is not to be believed that a person of such comprehensive views as Jesus Christ could have fallen into so manifest a contradiction as to assert that men would be tortured after death by that Being whose character is held up as a model to human kind, because He is incapable of malevolence and revenge. All the arguments which have been brought forward to justify retribution fail, when retribution is destined neither to operate as an example to other agents nor to the offender himself.'[1]

The news of the death of Princess Charlotte, and the news of the execution of Brandreth, Ludlow, and Turner for high treason, reached Shelley about the same time. The execution drew forth the passionate anger of the poet. He imagines the victims awaiting the last moment.[2] ' Hell is before their eyes, and they shudder and feel sick with fear lest some unrepented

[1] *Prose Works*, vol. i., p. 262–71.
[2] Ibid., vol. ii., p. 111.   Shelley's ' Address to the People on the Death of the Princess Charlotte,' by the ' Hermit of Marlowe,' was published in 1817.

or some wilful sin should seal their doom in everlasting fire.'

Canto VIII. of Shelley's lengthy narrative poem, called, in later editions, ' The Revolt of Islam,' discusses the nature of the Power that rules the universe, and we find in sub-section viii. the following :

> And it is said this Power will punish wrong;
> Yes, add despair to crime, and pain to pain !
> And deepest hell and deathless snakes among
> Will bind the wretch on whom is fixed a stain
> Which like a plague, a burden, and a bane,
> Clung to him while he lived ;

and again in Canto X., sub-section xxxv. :

> . . . When we are dead, the day
> Of judgement comes, and all shall surely know
> Whose God is God, each fearfully shall pay
> The errors of his faith in endless woe !

Even then the horrible thought cannot be left, for Shelley writes (xxxvii.) :

> Ay, there is famine in the gulf of hell,
> Its giant worms of fire for ever yawn—
> Their lurid eyes are on us ! Those who fell
> By the swift shafts of pestilence ere dawn
> Are in their jaws ! They hunger for the spawn
> Of Satan.

Then follows a description of hell too long to be quoted here, but one which surely must out-Herod Herod in its horror.

We pass on to the poem ' Rosalind and Helen ' (1819), only to find borne out our suggestion that Shelley can scarcely write any poem or essay without some reference to hell. So here :

> She is adulterous, and doth hold
> In secret that the Christian creed
> Is false, and therefore is much need
> That I should have a care to save
> My children from eternal fire.

SHELLEY

And again :

> The ministers of misrule sent,
> Seized upon Lionel, and bore
> His chained limbs to a dreary tower,
> In the midst of a city vast and wide.
> For he, they said, from his mind had bent
> Against their gods keen blasphemy,
> For which, though his soul must roasted be
> In hell's red lakes immortally,
> Yet even on earth must he abide
> The vengeance of their slaves.

' The Cenci ' (1819) is a characteristically Shelleyan subject, dealing, as its author loved to do, with tyranny oppressing innocence, appearing to triumph, and yet suffering defeat in a spiritual sense. Count Francesco Cenci is such a tyrant that his daughter, Beatrice, cannot bear to think of God as a Father, for the latter word has, for her, lost its meaning.

Beatrice :

> If sometimes, as a shape more like himself,
> Even the form which tortured me on earth,
> Masked in grey hairs and wrinkles, he should come
> And wind me in his hellish arms, and fix
> His eyes on mine, and drag me down, down, down !
> For was he not alone omnipotent
> On Earth ? and ever present ? Even tho' dead,
> Does not his spirit live in all that breathe,
> And work for me and mine still the same ruin,
> Scorn, pain, despair ? Who ever yet returned
> To teach the laws of death's untrodden realm ?
> Unjust perhaps as those which drive us now,
> Oh, whither, whither ?

Lucretia :

>   Trust in God's sweet love,
> The tender promises of Christ : ere night,
> Think, we shall be in Paradise.

(Act V., sc. 4.)

Note also the words of Lucretia about Giacomo, who, she says,

> ... will find
> Life a worse hell than that beyond the grave.

So the conception of hell, which we suggest was an obsession, is ready to rise to Shelley's mind, not only in a philosophic poem, but in a magnificent drama like 'The Cenci.'

When we turn to 'Prometheus Unbound,' written at Rome in the spring of 1819 and published in 1820, we see a conception of the hopelessness of punishment and torture as an answer to belief and liberty of thought.

> *Prometheus* :
> I would not quit
> This bleak ravine, these unrepentant pains.
> *Mercury* :
> Alas! I wonder at, yet pity thee.
> *Prometheus* :
> Pity the self despising slaves of Heaven
> Not me, within whose mind sits peace serene
> As light in the sun.

And later in the poem we find (Act II., sc. iv.) Asia arraigning God as the creator of hell and 'the sharp fear of hell.'

The idea of hell is not developed in 'Oedipus Tyrannus' or in 'Epipsychidion,' though the idea of tyranny is present in both, and receives what it is bound to receive at Shelley's hands—contempt and derision. Hell's sulphurous fumes do not mar the quiet dignity of what, to the writer, is the finest of all Shelley's poems, 'Adonais.' Nor does the obsession mar the last work issued during Shelley's life, 'Hellas.'

The poems we shall consider now were published as *Posthumous Poems* in 1824, two years after his death, though in date of composition many of them precede those already discussed. In the fragment, 'Prince Athanase,' we find this significant passage:

> Nor what religion fables of the grave
> Feared he.

In 'Peter Bell the Third,' written in 1819, we hear the flames of Shelley's hell crackling brightly:

> Peter Bell,
> Damned since our first parents fell,
> Damned eternally to Hell—
> Surely he deserves it well!
>
> And Peter Bell, when he had been
> With fresh imported Hell-fire warmed,
> Grew serious . . . ;

with a good deal more on the subject of hell-fire and damnation, including the lines:

> And this is Hell—and in this smother
> All are damnable and damned;
> Each one damning, damns the other;
> They are damned by one another,
> By none other are they damned.
> 'Tis a lie to say, 'God damns!'

In the drama of 'Charles the First' we find the prisoner, Bastwick, who is condemned to

> pay five thousand
> Pounds to the king, lose both his ears, be branded
> With red hot iron on the cheek and forehead,

addressing his judges in the Star Chamber thus:

> Were I an enemy of my God and King
> And of good men, as ye are ;—I should merit
> Your fearful state and gilt prosperity,
> Which, when ye wake from the last sleep, shall turn
> To cowls and robes of everlasting fire.

In the poem, 'To the Lord Chancellor,' Shelley, tortured in soul, breaks out in curses upon Lord Eldon, who decided that the poet was not a fit person to have charge of his own children by Harriet Westbrook, and ordered that they should be left in the charge of a certain Church of England clergyman:

> By the false cant which on their innocent lips
> Must hang like poison on an opening bloom,
> By the dark creeds which cover with eclipse
> Their pathway from the cradle to the tomb—
> By thy most impious Hell, and all its terror;
> .   .   .   .
> I curse thee.

Among the latest poems published were ' The Masque of Anarchy ' (published in 1832) and ' The Daemon of the World ' (1876), and in both we find traces of the intense feeling which the poet had against a system which could contain such conceptions as the current one about hell. In the first lines are found:

> Freemen never
> Dream that God will damn for ever
> All who think those things untrue
> Of which Priests make such ado.
>   (lviii.)

In the second we find a line about

> The bloodhound of religion's hungry zeal.

In his essay *Speculations on Morals* (published in 1833), Shelley shows at length how corrupted the conception of morality became when linked to it was the thought of the eternal torments of hell,[1] and in his *Essay on the Devil and on Devils* we find him tilting at the same anomaly : ' To tempt mankind to incur everlasting damnation must, on the part of God, and even on the part of the Devil, arise from that disinterested love of tormenting and annoying which is seldom observed on

---
[1] *Prose Works*, ed. Forman, vol. ii., p. 314.

earth. The thing that comes nearest to it is a troop of idle, dirty boys baiting a cat; cooks skinning eels and boiling lobsters alive and bleeding calves and whipping pigs to death; naturalists anatomizing dogs alive... are nothing compared to God and the Devil, judging, damning, and then tormenting the soul of a miserable sinner.'[1]

We have now searched every known work of Shelley's and found that in every one up to 1820 there is some noticeable result of what we have called the 'hell complex.' We do not wish to overestimate this finding. Indeed, it is merely the religious aspect of Shelley's two master passions—the passion for justice and the passion for sincerity. But it is significant, and we believe it to be the best example in the world of the great harm wrought by bad thinking, and of forcing the result of such bad thinking—under the name of religious teaching—on the followers of such a person as Jesus Christ. In the last two years of Shelley's life the fires of his hell died down and the smoke no longer obscured his vision; but we have gathered enough evidence to show how that false and vulgar conception poisoned that sincere mind and horrified that tender spirit.

We must go farther yet, however, to understand the far-reaching effect of this complex. We must not judge its effect on Shelley's nature by its effect on our own. The poet is always far more sensitive to injustice, cruelty, and oppression than the ordinary man. Quotations might be made from every poet, but we must realize that in Shelley we have a man whose nature was peculiarly and abnormally sensitive. We shall then be in a position to understand, and to some extent measure, his reaction to the idea of hell.

Little circumstances affected Shelley to an extent which a more prosaic soul can hardly realize. When the poet was first married to Harriet Westbrook, Hogg, who lived with them in Edinburgh, tells us that the little maid who waited on them offended Shelley

[1] *Prose Works*, vol. ii., p. 394.

68 THE AFTER-WORLD OF THE POETS

merely on account of her Northern accent. ' " Send her away, Harriet," he would cry, rushing wildly into a corner and covering his face with his hands. " Oh, send her away ; for God's sake, send her away.[1] " '

In his *Speculations on Metaphysics*, Shelley is describing the not uncommon experience of being confronted with a scene which seems familiar to one, though one cannot actually remember having seen it before. Sometimes one has dreamed of it, and is, at a later date, startled to see it in actuality. Shelley, speaking of such an occurrence, described the view—a windmill enclosed within stone walls, standing in a meadow near Oxford. He describes the nature of the ground—' the long low hill behind the windmill, and a grey covering of uniform cloud spread over the evening sky. Then,' he adds, ' the effect which it produced on me was not such as could have been expected. I suddenly remembered to have seen that exact scene in some dream. . . . ' Then, after an obvious break in the manuscript, there follows the sentence, ' Here I was obliged to leave off, overcome by thrilling horror.' And there the manuscript, from which the fragment was given in 1840, closes. Mrs. Shelley thus comments upon it : ' I remember well his coming to me from writing it, pale and agitated, to seek refuge in conversation from the fearful emotions it excited.' Few men have had such keen susceptibility as Shelley. ' His nervous temperament was wound up by the delicacy of his health to an intense degree of sensibility, and while his active mind pondered for ever upon, and drew conclusions from, his sensations, his reveries increased their vivacity, till they mingled with, and were one with, thought, and both became absorbing and tumultuous, even to physical pain.'[2]

We shall give one more illustration of his abnormal sensitiveness, because it illustrates his reaction to the

[1] Dowden, *Life of Shelley*, vol. i., p. 180.
[2] *Prose Works*, vol. ii., p. 297.

horrible. Byron, Shelley, and Mrs. Shelley, on June 18, 1816, were sitting round the fire at Byron's house at Diodati, Italy, telling ghost stories. Byron tried to lift the theme of their talk to the higher regions of poetry. In order to do this he began to recite certain lines of Coleridge's poem, 'Christabel,' just published by Murray, which, though a copy had not reached him, Byron had read in manuscript and heard recited by its author. The lines he repeated included those which describe the horrible appearance of the witch:

> Then, drawing in her breath aloud
> Like one that shuddered, she unbound
> The cincture from beneath her breast:
> Her silken robe, and inner vest,
> Dropt to her feet, and full in view,
> Behold! her bosom and half her side—
> Hideous, deformed, and pale of hue.[1]
> A sight to dream of, not to tell!
> And she is to sleep by Christabel.[2]

When silence ensued,' wrote Polidori—a doctor half English and half Italian, who accompanied Byron— 'Shelley, suddenly shrieking and putting his hands to his head, ran out of the room with a candle. I threw water on his face and gave him ether. He was looking at Mrs. Shelley and suddenly thought of a woman he had heard of who had eyes instead of nipples; which, taking hold of his mind, horrified him.'[3]

We have only to add this extreme and abnormal sensitiveness to what we have seen to be the other qualities of Shelley's mind, to realize how deeply the obsession of hell influenced him. It bit into his soul like acid. We can see now the reason of his deep bitterness concerning certain aspects of religion, in the name of which the most pitiless persecutions which disgrace the pages of history have been carried out. We

[1] This line seems to have been omitted in later editions.
[2] This line in later editions reads,
    'O shield her! shield sweet Christabel.'
[3] Quoted by Dowden, *Life of Shelley*, vol. ii., p. 34.

can understand his hatred of priests, so marked a feature of all his writing.

Having viewed the destructive attack Shelley made on the crude conception of hell, we have yet to ask what constructive contribution he made to eschatalogical ideas. Was it only destructively that he dealt with so-called Christian conceptions, or did his whole scheme of an after-world embody what is best in Christian thinking on the subject? Did he, on the other hand, break away entirely from the Christian belief concerning immortality, and draw his materials from other sources? These are the questions to which we must now address ourselves.

It is interesting to notice, in examining the poet's constructive scheme of an after-world, that Shelley quotes the authority of Jesus Christ for some kind of life beyond the grave. 'It appears,' he says in his *Essay on Christianity*, ' that we moulder to a heap of senseless dust, to a few worms that arise and perish like ourselves. Jesus Christ asserts that these appearances are fallacious, and that a gloomy and cold imagination alone suggests the conception that thought can cease to be. Another and more extensive state of being will follow from that mysterious change which we call death.' Further essays, on *The Punishment of Death* and *On a Future State*, might be quoted in support of the contention that Shelley believes in immortality; but we believe that the quotation above shows us the nearest approach Shelley ever made to a Christian foundation for the superstructure of his thought on the subject.

When we turn to the poems we find a great deal of imagery which is very beautiful, but which, by its very vagueness, cannot be quoted as substantiating this or that view of the life after death. Take the following from ' Queen Mab ' :

> Death is a gate of dreariness and gloom
> That leads to azure isles and beaming skies,

And happy regions of eternal hope.
Therefore, O Spirit! fearlessly bear on.

. . . .

Fear not then, Spirit, death's disrobing hand.

. . . .

'Tis but the voyage of a darksome hour,
The transient gulph-dream of a startling sleep.
Death is no foe to virtue.[1]

And these from ' Prometheus Unbound ' :

death shall be the last embrace of her
Who takes the life she gave, even as a mother
Folding her child, says, ' Leave me not again.'

And again :

Death is the veil which those who live call life ;
They sleep, and it is lifted.

The idea of death as a mother occurs again in ' The Cenci,' when Beatrice says :

Come, obscure Death,
And wind me in thine all-embracing arms !
Like a fond mother hide me in thy bosom,
And rock me to the sleep from which none wake.

' Adonais ' is, of course, the *locus classicus* of the idea of immortality in Shelley ; though we are inclined to think that the most important contribution Shelley made to eschatology was his exposure of the false view of hell. In ' Adonais,' Shelley never mentions hell, nor, we think, does he come anywhere near the Christian conception of life after death. Yet there is a definite conception that Keats has survived the ordeal of death. The lines addressed, in the early part of the poem, to Urania, do not doubt immortality :

Oh, dream not that the amorous Deep
Will yet restore him to the vital air ;
Death feeds on his mute voice, and laughs at our despair ;

for we take it that the words ' vital air ' refer to earthly existence.

[1] The same lines occur in ' The Daemon of the World.'

The lines beginning:

> He will awake no more, oh, never more!

must, we think, be interpreted in the same way.

Some of the lines in 'Adonais' might be claimed to express the conception of *personal* immortality:

> Peace, peace! he is not dead, he doth not sleep—
> He hath awakened from the dream of life.
>
> . . . .
>
> He lives, he wakes—'Tis Death is dead, not he.

And personal immortality seems to us involved in the further conception that a thinking being cannot perish, and that man only learns the true secret of being, only gathers the true nature of happiness and the true glory of the eternal world, when this earthly life is broken up. So we have the passage (xx.):

> Naught we know, dies. Shall that alone which knows
> Be as a sword consumed before the sheath
> By sightless lightning?

and the famous passage (lii.):

> The One remains, the many change and pass;
> Heaven's light forever shines, Earth's shadows fly;
> Life, like a dome of many-coloured glass,
> Stains the white radiance of Eternity,
> Until Death tramples it to fragments.

Yet, though these extracts show a conception of immortality which may be regarded as personal, Shelley's thought is predominantly pantheistic:

> The pure spirit shall flow
> Back to the burning fountain whence it came,
> A portion of the Eternal.
> (xxxviii.)
>
> . . . .
>
> Thou, young Dawn
> Turn all thy dew to splendour, for from thee
> The spirit thou lamentest is not gone;
> (xli.)

> He is made one with Nature : there is heard
> His voice in all her music, from the moan
> Of thunder to the song of night's sweet bird ;
> He is a presence to be felt and known
> In darkness and in light, from herb and stone,
> Spreading itself where'er that Power may move
> Which has withdrawn his being to its own ;
> (xlii.)

> He is a portion of the loveliness
> Which once he made more lovely.
> (xliii.)

> The soft sky smiles,—the low wind whispers near ;
> 'Tis Adonais calls !
> (liii.)

Again he speaks of
> that sustaining Love
> Which through the web of being blindly wove
> By man and beast and earth and air and sea,
> Burns bright or dim, as each are mirrors of
> The fire for which all thirst.
> (liv.)

Our suggestion that the predominant thought in Adonais' is pantheistic finds some confirmation in the discovery that pantheistic thought colours Shelley's ideas of the life after death as expressed in other poems. In 'Alastor' we have the lines :

> But thou art fled
> Like some frail exhalation ; which the dawn
> Robes in its golden beams ;

and in 'Epipsychidion' :

> The spirit of the worm beneath the sod,
> In love and worship, blends itself with God.

and in the perfect 'Ode to the West Wind' :

> Be thou, spirit fierce,
> My spirit ! Be thou me, impetuous one !

When we remember, further, that Shelley was a great lover of Plato, we are not surprised to find pantheistic tendencies in his thought, since it would be difficult indeed to separate nineteenth-century Platonism from nineteenth-century pantheism. Some writers would make Shelley's religion entirely Platonic. It is 'Platonic' both in its excellencies and in what some might term its defects. Shelley, like Plato, believes in a supreme Power; it is beyond and above the world, but also within; at once immanent and transcendent; it works from within the world, struggling with the obstruction of matter, transforming matter, and moulding it to its will. Like Plato, Shelley is vividly conscious of the unity of the world and of all life; and the underlying spirit, though it reveals itself in many forms, is everywhere essentially the same. Plato contemplates it sometimes as the One in distinction to the many (*Parmenides*), sometimes as the supreme Good rising above all lesser goods (*Phaedrus*), sometimes as the supreme Wisdom (*Symposium*), sometimes as the supreme Beauty above all lesser beauties (*Phaedrus*). Shelley, too, celebrates this spirit in many ways. With him also it is the One in contradistinction to the many:

> The One remains, the many change and pass.

It is immanent in the world and yet transcendent. It is that power

> Which wields the world with never wearied love,
> Sustains it from beneath, and kindles it above.[1]

Shelley's admiration for Plato is manifest through his work. One recalls that Shelley made translations of some of Plato's writings; that in the Preface to 'Prometheus Unbound' he writes: 'For my part, I had rather be damned with Plato and Lord Bacon, than go to heaven with Paley and Malthus'; and the

[1] *Essays and Studies by Members of the English Association*, collected by Professor C. H. Herford, vol. iv., pp. 76–7.

original 'Prologue to Hellas' contains a reference to
> Plato's sacred light,
> Of which my spirit was a burning morrow.

Certainly there are many traces in Shelley of the Platonic ideas concerning immortality. The idea of reminiscence, of which we have spoken in regard to Wordsworth, has certainly influenced Shelley in the lines of ' Prince Athanase ' :
> Memories of an ante-natal life
> Made this, where now he dwelt, a penal hell;

and in the lines in ' Epipsychidion,' where Shelley says of certain memories :
> They seem
> Like echoes of an ante-natal dream.

Emilia is a winged soul, soaring over the darkness of earth, an incarnation of a brighter beauty, descending from a lovelier and more wondrous world,
> Veiling beneath that radiant form of Woman
> All that is insupportable in thee
> Of light, and love, and immortality !

The influence of Plato is discernible, we think, in the suggestions of pre-existence in ' Queen Mab,' where Shelley speaks of
> that strange state
> Before the naked soul has found its home ;

in ' Rosalind and Helen,' where, in regard to a baby, he speaks of searching
> the depths of its fair eyes
> For long-departed memories ;

and in ' Epipsychidion ' as follows :
> O too late,
> Belovèd ! O, too soon adored by me !
> For in the fields of immortality
> My spirit should at first have worshipped thine.

The idea of reincarnation in ' Hellas ' is taken, we think, from *Phaedo* :

> They are still immortal
> Who, through birth's orient portal
> And death's dark chasm hurrying to and fro,
>   Clothe their unceasing flight
>   In the brief dust and light
> Gathered around their chariots as they go.

The Platonic idea of the immortal nature of thought, and of the beauties of Nature as only blurred manifestations of a beauty of thought which is eternal, and only to be appreciated by the eye of the soul, is found repeatedly in Shelley. So in ' Hellas ' :

> Earth and ocean,
> Space, and the isles of life and light that gem
> The sapphire floods of interstellar air ;
> This firmament pavilioned upon chaos ;
>   .   .   .   .
>   this Whole
> Of suns, and worlds, and men, and beasts, and flowers
>   .   .   .   .
> Is but a vision . . .
> Thought is its cradle and its grave, nor less
> The future and the past are idle shadows
> Of thought's eternal flight—they have no being :
> Naught is, but that which feels itself to be.

And again :

> Thought
> Alone, and its quick elements, Will, Passion,
> Reason, Imagination, cannot die ;
> They are, what that which they regard appears,
> The stuff whence mutability can weave
> All that it hath dominion o'er.

The same idea is suggested in ' Prometheus Unbound ' :

> For know there are two worlds of life and death :
> One that which thou beholdest ; but the other
> Is underneath the grave, where do inhabit
> The shadows of all forms that think and live
> Till death unite them and they part no more.

We have quoted enough to show that, though Shelley made destructive criticisms of certain points of contemporary theology, when he came to construct his after-world he borrowed his conceptions from Plato rather than from the New Testament. There is not one idea which is distinctively Christian in Shelley's thought of immortality; and we think it is not too much to say that Shelley thus broke away from Christian thought because he was outraged by the current conceptions of the after-life in which unjust punishment played so large a part. He had 'no quarrel with Jesus Christ,' one of his biographers tells us; and Browning said definitely, ' I shall say what I think—had Shelley lived, he would have finally ranged himself with the Christians '[1]; and we remarked that in later poems Shelley regretted some passages in ' Queen Mab ' and ceased to rave against the forms of Christian belief, even those expressed in terms which a poet could not but regard as crude. However, except to criticize it, Shelley nowhere comes near the definite Christian view of life beyond the grave.[2]

Francis Thompson, once for all, has pointed out the unsatisfactory nature, from a philosophic point of view, of Shelley's after-world : ' What utter desolation can it be that discerns comfort in this hope, whose wan countenance is as the countenance of despair ? . . . What deepest depth of agony is it that finds consolation in this immortality : an immortality which thrusts you into death, the maw of Nature, that your dissolved elements may circulate through her veins ?

' Yet such, the poet tells me, is my sole balm for the hurts of life. I am as the vocal breath floating from an organ. I, too, shall fade on the winds, a cadence soon forgotten. So I dissolve and die, and am lost in the ears of men : the particles of my being twine in newer

[1] *Essay on Shelley*, p. 78.

[2] ' One thing prevents " Adonais " from being ideally perfect : its lack of Christian hope.'—*Collected Works of Francis Thompson*, vol. iii., p. 28.

melodies, and from my one death arise a hundred lives. Why, through the thin partition of this consolation pantheism can hear the groans of its neighbour pessimism. Better almost the black resignation which the fatalist draws from his own hopelessness, from the fierce kisses of misery that hiss against his tears.'[1]

Matthew Arnold has likened Shelley to a 'beautiful and ineffectual angel, beating in the void his luminous wings in vain.' 'Beautiful' is a word which no one who has read Shelley's poems would deem unfitting. Moreover, the figure of an angel with luminous wings is apt enough. There is something very spiritual about Shelley. There is something about his poetry as dream-like and unearthly as the Taj Mahal seen in moonlight. If we accept the words 'ineffectual' and 'in vain,' it should be with the reservation that what made Shelley 'ineffectual,' and his work 'in vain,' was not his passionate message of freedom and justice, of liberty and charity in thought and act, but rather the blind stupidity of his contemporaries, who could not accept it because of the hardness of their hearts; who wrapped the garments of their own conventions of thought and habit about them, and drew away from Shelley as from a leper.

It is ever the way of humanity to persecute those deliverers who would help it to rise from the rut which is rapidly deepening into a grave, and then call them 'ineffectual' and their work 'vain.' If only men had looked and listened and heeded, they would have found in Shelley a visionary and a prophet who would have led them far; who would have broken from their limbs the shackles of too rigid convention, effete belief, bigoted persecution, and pitiless intolerance; who would have lifted them to those high altitudes of the spirit where the winds of freedom, love, and liberty blow; where men hear the voice of God and look upon His face.

[1] Francis Thompson, op. cit., vol. iii., p. 29.

III

A NEW PROJECTION OF CHRISTIAN THOUGHT BORN OF THE FEAR OF DEATH

III

A NEW PROJECTION OF CHRISTIAN THOUGHT BORN OF THE FEAR OF DEATH[1]

TENNYSON, 1809-1892

WHEN we come to discuss the idea of immortality in Tennyson we find ourselves in a very different atmosphere from that which surrounds us when we make the same quest in the poetry of Wordsworth and Shelley. Two factors emerge. In the first place, Tennyson's vision is coloured to a much greater extent by Christian thought. In the second place, the world which listened to his poetry was no longer a world dozing amid its accepted religious orthodoxies, and banning, as outside the pale, any who dared to dispute them. It was a world of unrest and confusion, a world frightened and whimpering with its fear, a world distraught by the spectacle of the discoveries of science, apparently destroying the cherished 'fundamentals' of religion. These two facts partly account for the immense popularity which Tennyson enjoyed. With all his faults, which a certain school of critics is most anxious that we should realize, it must at least be said that, with praiseworthy intellectual honesty, Tennyson welcomed every new finding of science—

>   Yearning in desire
> To follow knowledge like a sinking star,
> Beyond the utmost bound of human thought—[2]

[1] An article on 'Tennyson's After-World,' by the present writer, and written as a preliminary study for the section of this chapter dealing with 'In Memoriam' appeared in the *London Quarterly Review* in October 1925. A lecture on the same subject was delivered to the Manchester Poetical Society in the Houldsworth Hall, Manchester, March 19, 1925.
[2] 'Ulysses.'

and that he was able, in a manner comforting and convincing to hosts of his readers, to co-ordinate and harmonize the new knowledge with what he regarded as the essentials of the old faith.

These two factors are, we think, important enough to deserve fuller treatment. We do not mean to imply that Tennyson's thought is bounded on all sides by the Christian creeds. A poet can never be thus bound and remain a poet. At the same time, a careful reading of the famous *Memoir* and the whole of the poems, many of which speak over and over again of Christ,[1] does, we think, justify the contention that the Christian religion influenced the poet's mind to a greater degree than any other influence, such, for instance, as that of Platonism.

Mr. A. C. Benson, in his book on the poet, seems to us unduly disturbed by the lack of Christian teaching in ' In Memoriam.' He says, ' With every wish to find a definite Christian faith expressed in " In Memoriam," I must confess that I certainly cannot discover it there.'[2] We agree with Mr. Benson in the sense that Tennyson has not built up his scheme from materials all of which are found within the Christian dogmas. Scientific thought, as we shall see, contributed largely to the scheme. On the other hand, we think it may fairly be claimed that Tennyson's scheme may be accepted by the Christian as that kind of projection of thought which, without contradicting the implicit dogmas of Christianity, goes further than Christian thought has yet ventured. As Mr. Benson says, ' the whole poem is, of course, instinct with strong Christian feeling throughout ' ; and we wonder whether a poem could be more than this, however determined its author was on writing a Christian poem, since there is such a paucity of accepted dogma on this subject.

---

[1] ' In Memoriam,' ' The Coming of Arthur,' ' Gareth and Lynette,' ' Guinevere.'

[2] *Tennyson*, p. 173.

Mr. Benson finds a difficulty in the absence of any reference to the Resurrection. We think it must be admitted that Tennyson's own faith was not built up only of materials included in Christianity. He was one

> Whose faith has centre everywhere,
> Nor cares to fix itself to form.

At the same time, we need not suppose that Tennyson did not believe in the continued existence of Jesus Christ after death. No one who did not believe in Christ's survival of bodily death could write these lines:

> Thy spirit should fail from off the globe;
> . . . .
> What time mine own might also flee,
> . . . .
> And He that died in Holy Land
> Would reach us out the shining hand,
> And take us as a single soul.[1]

It may well be that Tennyson did not bind himself to any specific theory of the Resurrection; but survival, not its manner, is surely the essential element in the Christian dogma; and it seems to us unwarranted to refuse the word 'Christian' to the whole poem for lack of references to the manner in which the soul may survive the shock of death—admittedly a subject on which the most daring thinkers both in poetry and philosophy walk with careful steps. We know, moreover, how careful the poet was not to use terms which

---

[1] Note the passage in 'The Holy Grail' when the King speaks of moments when a man
> 'feels he cannot die,
> And knows himself no vision to himself,
> Nor the high God a vision, nor that One
> Who rose again.'

might be construed to carry more than he himself meant.[1]

'It is impossible,' says Mr. Benson, 'that one who was a Christian in the strictest sense should not have recurred again and again to this thought in a poem which deals from first to last with death and hope.' We do not agree.

We suggest that there is another reason for the omission which Mr. Benson so deplores. Tennyson probably felt that there is no reason to suppose that *because* Christ overcame death we shall do the same. The idea of immortality receives strong *confirmation* from the experience of Jesus Christ, but not proof. There can be no proof of immortality. Modern Christian teachers are ready to admit that one cannot argue from Christ's survival to our own.[2] Nor do we think that Tennyson's after-world should be called non-Christian simply because he does not draw his evidence from the data of the Christian faith which we regard as convincing. We should not ask that a poet should build up an argument. We ask him to show us a vision.

Any poet might say, with the maiden in 'The Palace of Art,'

> I take possession of man's mind and deed.
> I care not what the sects may brawl.
> I sit as God holding no form of creed,
> But contemplating all.

[1] Note as characteristic his refusal to receive Holy Communion in his study at Freshwater in 1892 save in the simplest sense. He quoted his own lines ('Queen Mary,' Act IV., sc. 2):
'It is but a communion, not a mass—
No sacrifice, but a life-giving feast.'

[2] See Professor H. R. Mackintosh, *Immortality and the Future*, pp. 178-9. Dr. G. Galloway, *Baird Lecture for* 1917, p. 8: 'To those who are sceptical of future life it would be useless to urge the resurrection of Christ as a proof.' See also F. C. S. Schiller, *Riddles of the Sphinx*, p. 373: 'It is impossible to argue from the bodily resurrection of a divine being to the survival of the soul of ordinary men.' See also the present writer's *After Death*, p. 16 et seq.

For ourselves, we should be content to say that the influence of Christian teaching is a more potent force than any other which moulds the poet's conception of an after-world.

This should not blind us to the fact that other influences are discernible. Section cxxx. in 'In Memoriam' sounds as pantheistic as sections of 'Adonais.'

> Thy voice is on the rolling air;
>   I hear thee where the waters run;
>   Thou standest in the rising sun,
> And in the setting thou art fair.
>
> What art thou then? I cannot guess;
>   But tho' I seem in star and flower
>   To feel thee some diffusive power,
> I do not therefore love thee less:
>
> My love involves the love before;
>   My love is vaster passion now;
>   Tho' mixed with God and Nature thou,
> I seem to love thee more and more.
>
> Far off thou art, but ever nigh;
>   I have thee still, and I rejoice;
>   I prosper, circled with thy voice;
> I shall not lose thee tho' I die.

It would be absurd to suggest that the above stanza is not most readily interpreted as pantheistic. Yet when one remembers who wrote it one wonders whether there is not an alternative interpretation, though we have not seen this suggestion made, and the commentators would seem not to allow it. Nature, to many poetic souls, is a door into the world of spiritual realities. To some poets, as we have seen, the beauties of nature are but shadows cast by the splendour of those spiritual realities of which they are an imperfect manifestation. It is possible, we think, that, to Tennyson, Hallam belonged to the kingdom of the spiritual, to that real world of spiritual beauty to which nature so imperfectly sought to lead men's souls. If this were so, any experience which made the spiritual more real made the friend who lived in the spiritual more real also. Nay, might not the loveliness of nature which linked him to the spiritual world link him also with that friend who dwelt within it? This is not a strange idea in poetry. Poets with far less poetical discernment have had this mystic experience.

> And sometimes in the twilight gloom apart
> The tall trees whisper, heart to heart;
> From my fond lips the eager answers fall,
> Thinking I hear thee call.

May not the second and third verses of the stanza quoted from ' In Memoriam ' mean that though the friend has entered the infinite world of spiritual beauty; though he has lost, perhaps, a distinctiveness which was his in the body; though every beauty of nature seems to be capable of acting as a medium to bring Hallam's spirit near to his own, until the friend seems ' mixed with God and nature '—yet his love remains the same.

A letter of Coventry Patmore, written in August 1850, is interesting in discussing the possible presence of the influence of pantheistic thought in ' In Memoriam.' ' He is far above all the pantheistic " religious faculty " humbug that taints so many half-geniuses in this day; and I am sure that he would be horrified if he knew that any such men had been led by " In Memoriam " to count him as a fellow heathen.'

We find very few references to Platonic influence in Tennyson's work. This, it has been said, is due to his limitations. He does not seem, at any rate, to have been deeply interested in technical philosophy, though he was very fond of philosophical speculation. On one occasion he said, ' I have but a gleam of Kant, and have hardly turned a page of Hegel'; and though in the *Memoir* there are references to his reading Aeschylus, Euripides, and Homer in Greek, there is no reference to his reading Plato in Greek, though he derived much pleasure from receiving from Jowett his translation of Plato in four volumes, and presumably read them.

There are some passages in his poems which remind us irresistibly of Plato. Take, for example, the following from ' De Profundis ' :

> Out of the deep, my child, out of the deep,
> From that great deep, before our world begins,
> Whereon the spirit of God moves as he will—
> Out of the deep, my child, out of the deep,
> *From that true world within the world we see,*
> *Whereof our world is but the bounding shore—*
> Out of the deep, Spirit, out of the deep,
> With this ninth moon, that sends the hidden sun
> Down yon dark sea, thou comest, darling boy ;

or the passage in ' The Ancient Sage,' where the younger man throws doubt on the idea of immortality, saying,

> O worms and maggots of to-day,
> Without their hope of wings
> . . . . . .
> Tho' some have gleams or so they say,
> Of more than mortal things.

The reply of the sage brings us very near Plato, for he finds his answer not in ' to-day,' but in an alleged vague memory of pre-natal life.

> To-day ? but what of yesterday ? for oft
> On me, when boy, there came what then I call'd,
> Who knew no books and no philosophies,
> In my boy phrase, ' The Passion of the Past,'
> The first grey streak of earliest summer-dawn,
> The last long stripe of waning crimson gloom,

> As if the late and early were but one—
> A height, a broken grange, a grove, a flower
> Had murmurs, 'Lost and gone and lost and gone!'
> A breath, a whisper—some divine farewell—
> Desolate sweetness—far and far away—
> What had he loved, what had he lost, the boy?
> I know not, and I speak of what has been.

Tennyson returns to the same idea in a still later poem called 'Far-Far-Away.'

> A whisper from his dawn of life? a breath
> From some fair dawn beyond the doors of death,
>   Far-far-away?
>
> Far, far, how far? from o'er the gates of Birth,
> The faint horizons, all the bounds of earth,
>   Far-far-away?

There are possible echoes of Plato in the first of the 'Early Sonnets,' beginning,

> As when with downcast eyes we muse and brood,
> And ebb into a former life;

and in the lines on the 'Two Voices,'

> Moreover, something is or seems,
> That touches me with mystic gleams,
> Like glimpses of forgotten dreams—

but the references are too vague to need lengthy quotation or comment.

These are the only passages in Tennyson which show the influence of Platonic *thought*. Professor Mustard[1] has collected a number of allusions to Plato such as that in 'Lucretius'—

> lend an ear to Plato where he says
> That men like soldiers may not quit their post
> Allotted by the Gods—

[1] *Classical Echoes in Tennyson*, Professor W. P. Mustard.

which is an allusion to the *Phaedo* (62*b*), where the thought is expressed that men are on a kind of garrison duty from which they ought not to run away; but this is a mere allusion, not the adoption of a philosophic idea. Other similar allusions are scattered through Tennyson's work; but, as they do not affect his thought, they are not relevant to our quest.

We believe that it is in ' In Memoriam ' that we must look for the real Tennyson in regard to the subject of immortality. And here, even if the stanza already quoted be labelled ' pantheistic,' yet even then the pantheism of ' In Memoriam ' is not one per cent. of the whole of the poem. ' In Memoriam ' is written in the poet's life-blood. It is the poet's own soul crying out in the wilderness of sorrowful bereavement that we listen to here. It is important to notice also that, when questions were put to Tennyson about Christ, he would say to his son, ' Answer for me that I have given my belief in " In Memoriam." '[1] Here, on surer ground, what do we find? Christ is addressed as ' Strong Son of God, Immortal Love,' as the ' Life Indeed,' as ' Lord,' as the ' Word.' This seems to us the language of a Christian writer, and one recalls words from the *Memoir* which would seem to support the language of ' In Memoriam.' ' I am not very fond of creeds,' said the poet, ' but I know that God Himself came down from heaven in likeness of men.'

We must turn now to notice the influence of the new interest in science upon the idea of immortality as it is found in Tennyson; though, of course, not only this idea, but the whole of his later poetry was influenced by the new vogue of science.

The main scientific influence was that of the theory of evolution—' sounding watchword,' as Tennyson called it—which acted in two ways. In the first place, it was misregarded as an upward tendency which meant inevitable progress. It appeared that humanity

[1] *Memoir*, p. 272.

was in a kind of lift or elevator, and must 'move upward,' willy-nilly. Colour was lent to this misconception by the extraordinary applications of recent discoveries which characterized Tennyson's age. Science was to lighten the toil of man, remove his sufferings, cure his diseases, end his wretched social conditions, and in some dimly apprehended way secure his moral and mental enlightenment also. We are afraid that there are suggestions of this unbalanced view in ' Locksley Hall ' (1842—before the appearance of Darwin's book) :

Men my brothers, men the workers, ever reaping something new :
That which they have done but earnest of the things that they shall do.

Tennyson, strangely prophetic of the present century, sees

The heavens fill with commerce, argosies of magic sails,
Pilots of the purple twilight, dropping down with costly bales.

There are glimpses of a kind of League of Nations when he

Heard the heavens fill with shouting, and there rained a ghastly dew
From the nations' airy navies grappling in the central blue ;
. . . .
Till the war-drum throbb'd no longer, and the battle-flags were furled
In the Parliament of man, the Federation of the world ;

and thus the 'thoughts of men' widen with the general progress.

By the time ' Locksley Hall Sixty Years After ' was written (1886), the belief in inevitable progress has been sorely shattered. The old poet writes in cynical bitterness. He lost faith in the coming of the time

> When the schemes and all the systems, Kingdoms and Republics fall,
> Something kindlier, higher, holier—all for each and each for all?

He fears that he will not see

> All the full brain, half-brain races, led by Justice, Love, and Truth,
> All the millions one at length with all the visions of my youth?
>
> All diseases quenched by Science, no man halt, or deaf, or blind;
> Stronger ever born of weaker, lustier body, larger mind?
>
> Earth at last a warless world, a single race, a single tongue—
> I have seen her far away—for is not earth as yet so young?—
>
> Every tiger madness muzzled, every serpent passion kill'd,
> Every grim ravine a garden, every blazing desert till'd,
>
> Robed in universal harvest up to either pole she smiles,
> Universal ocean softly washing all her warless Isles.

In the second place the theory of evolution, as popularly conceived, appeared to draw man entirely within the natural order, even though he was still regarded as the culmination of the process of development. Darwin believed that man's conscience and emotions, as well as his physical body, came to him by descent from animal ancestors. Man was *entirely* a product of naturalistic evolution. Obviously this view influenced the idea of immortality to a very large extent. Man, on this hypothesis, was utterly insignificant. Well might Tennyson sing,

> What are men that He should heed us? cried the king of sacred song;
> Insects of an hour, that hourly work their brother insect wrong.

(Though this must not be understood as the poet's

final answer to the question raised.) It became almost impossible to many to accept this new finding of science and retain a faith in immortality.

Tennyson accepted with characteristic broad-mindedness the findings of responsible scientists; so much so that he was labelled the most scientific poet of his century. 'Scientific leaders like Herschel, Owen, Sedgwick, and Tyndall regarded him as a champion of science, and cheered him with words of genuine admiration for his love of nature, for the eagerness with which he welcomed all the latest scientific discoveries, for his trust in truth'; while 'men like Maurice and Robertson thought that the author had made a definite step towards the unification of the highest religion and philosophy with the progressive science of the day.'[1]

This harmonizing was not carried to a point which accepted a *purely* naturalistic view of life and man.

> I trust I have not wasted breath:
> I think we are not wholly brain,
>
> . . . . . .
>
> Not only cunning casts in clay:
> Let Science prove we are, and then
> What matters science unto men,
> At least to me? I would not stay.[2]

And again in 'Vastness':

What the philosophies, all the sciences, poesy, varying voices of prayer?
All that is noblest, all that is basest, all that is filthy with all that is fair?

What is it all, if we all of us end but in being our own corpse-coffins at last,
Swallowed in Vastness, lost in Silence, drown'd in the deeps of a meaningless Past?

What but a murmur of gnats in the gloom, or a moment's anger of bees in their hive?

[1] *Memoir*, p. 250. [2] 'In Memoriam,' cxx.

So, at a time when many lost their faith, when multitudes found their faith eclipsed, in an age of real spiritual agony, Tennyson clung ' ever to the sunnier side of doubt,' and to ' faith beyond the forms of faith,'[1] and showed a way out from the seeming impasse created by the ascertained facts of science on the one hand and the dogmas of revealed religion on the other. Stanza cxviii. of ' In Memoriam ' excellently illustrates this point, though certain lines of the stanza are obscure in meaning. The general drift, however, is that man's soul has not been produced only to perish, as have lower forms of life in bygone ages. Man is not only destined to advance to something higher on earth, but

>   those we call the dead
> Are breathers of an ampler day
> For ever nobler ends.

Nature never wastes a process, and the evolutionary process is not only designed to perfect man, as man, upon the earth, but to prepare him for a still vaster life, a preparation involving both the elements of growth and struggle. Thus the poet combats the idea that evolution is in the nature of a mechanical elevator. We are to work out the beast.

>   They say
> The solid earth whereon we tread
>
> In tracts of fluent heat began,
>   And grew to seeming-random forms,
>   The seeming prey of cyclic storms,
> Till at the last arose the man ;
>
> Who throve and branch'd from clime to clime,
>   The herald of a higher race,
>   And of himself in higher place,
> If so he type this work of time

[1] ' The Ancient Sage.'

> Within himself, from more to more,
>   Or crown'd with attributes of woe
>   Like glories, move his course, and show
> That life is not as idle ore,
>
> But iron dug from central gloom,
>   And heated hot with burning fears,
>   And dipt in baths of hissing tears,
> And batter'd with the shocks of doom
>
> To shape and use. Arise and fly
>   The reeling Faun, the sensual feast;
>   Move upward, working out the beast,
> And let the ape and tiger die.

In ' Maud ' Tennyson wrote,

As nine months go to the shaping an infant ripe for his birth,
So many a million of ages have gone to the making of man
He now is first, but is he the last?

And his own answer to the query was ' No, mankind is as yet on one of the lowest rungs of the ladder ' (Cf. ' The herald of a higher race '), ' although every man has, and has had from everlasting, his true and perfect being in the Divine Consciousness.'[1]

Tennyson was one of the first to realize that an acceptance of the doctrine of evolution did not necessarily militate against an acceptance of the then orthodox religious view of the origin of man. Given that the Genesis story is a kind of picture-parable designed to show God as the ultimate author of all creation—a story which was not intended, and which could not possibly claim, to be scientific—Tennyson showed that in the theory of evolution we have not an explanation of the origin of man which rules out the divine. We have a description of the methods used by the Divine Author. To satisfy himself on this point,

---

[1] *Memoir*, p. 272.

we find that on August 17, 1868, when Darwin called on Tennyson at Farringford, the poet said to the scientist, ' Your theory of evolution does not make against Christianity ? ' To which Darwin replied, ' No, certainly not.'[1]

Tennyson's ' By an Evolutionist ' (1888) gives us most completely his considered and final opinion on evolution. The whole poem might relevantly be quoted. We content ourselves with the final verse.

I have clim'd to the snows of Age, and I gaze at a field in the
  Past
Where I sank with the body at times in the sloughs of a low
  desire,
But I hear no yelp of the beast, and the Man is quiet at last
As he stands on the heights of his life with a glimpse of a
  height that is higher.

Thus evolution, as we have said, not only means the perfecting of men on earth, but it points to a further progress still, for which it has been a preparation, and which is its aim and culmination.

We are now in a position to pass on to notice the supreme importance of the idea of immortality in Tennyson's estimation. He is *the* poet of this idea in English. No other English poet has given the idea the pre-eminence which Tennyson gives to it. Present existence is to him hardly worth having if immortality be not true. The idea might be called, without exaggeration, the corner-stone of his edifice of thought. Obviously so superlative a claim will need substantiating.

In 1850, Tennyson said to Bishop Lightfoot, ' The cardinal point in Christianity is the life after death.'[2] Hallam Tennyson says of his father, ' I have heard him even say that he would rather know that he was to be lost eternally than not know that the whole human

[1] *Memoir*, p. 464.   [2] *Memoir*, p. 269. Cf. also pp. 416, 504.

race was to live eternally.' Again the poet is quoted as saying, ' I can hardly understand how any great imaginative man who has deeply lived, suffered, thought, and wrought, can doubt of the soul's continuous progress in the after-life. . . . If you allow a God, and God allows this strong instinct and universal yearning for another life, surely that is in a measure a presumption of its truth. We cannot give up the mighty hopes that make us men.'

So we are not susprised to hear him, writing in 1863 to a correspondent who has been bereaved, say, ' I sympathize with your grief, and, if faith means anything at all, it is trusting to those instincts, or feelings, or whatever they may be called, which assure us of some life after this.' Again he writes from Haslemere in 1871, ' I doubt whether I can bring you any solace, except by stating my own belief that the son, whom you so loved, is not really what we call dead, but more actually living than when alive here. . . . If it were not so, that which made us would seem too cruel a Power to be worshipped, and could not be loved.'

Passage after passage from the famous *Memoir* and from *Tennyson and His Friends* could be quoted to show the poet's beliefs on this subject, and the brisk discussions concerning it which he had with his friends. W. E. H. Lecky wrote to Hallam Lord Tennyson, ' Your father thought much about religious matters, and often dwelt with great force on his intuitive conviction of immortality with its corollaries of theism and Providence. Those beliefs he held very strongly, but they were, I think, wholly detached in his mind from the dogmas of particular creeds.' The poet was fond of telling the story of a certain Parisian who, having deliberately ordered and eaten a good dinner, committed suicide by covering his face with a chloroformed handkerchief. ' That is what I should do,' said the poet, ' if I thought there was no future life.'

Indeed, his whole conception of religion seems to find its centre in this question. In its truth other truths which might seem to outweigh it in importance, such as that of the Fatherhood of God, were, for the poet, included and contained. If this were not true, then, for Tennyson, Christianity was not true. There was no God in the universe at all, but only a mocking fiend. If immortality were a delusion, Tennyson would have agreed with the friend of Mark Twain who described all human history as a ' brief and rather discreditable episode on one of the minor planets.'

We wish now to ask why it was that the subject loomed so largely in the poet's mind, and we wish to offer tentatively two answers.

The first is that it proved an easy answer to a great many questions, a simple panacea for all sorts of ills, a facile solution for almost every problem. Tennyson will pat humanity on the head as one who says, ' Weep not now, for in a further life all ills will be put right, all pain and misery and sin will give place to pleasure and happiness, and all injustice will be adjusted.' There is a sense in which Tennyson offers immortality as a kind of bribe to the race. As he says in ' The Lover's Tale,' the discord of life here will be followed by

> that music which rights all

in the world to come. So in ' The Two Voices ' the poet faces the problem ' Is life worth living ? ' and his answer is ' Not unless it is continued.' We are urged to try to balance the evil in the world by setting forth

> that which might ensue
> With this old soul in organs new.

The ' Vision of Sin ' gives the poet another type of problem, but the answer is the same. Here sensual pleasure in youth has produced cynicism in age.

98   THE AFTER-WORLD OF THE POETS

Indulgence has vitiated the senses to such an extent that now, jaded and outworn, they can no longer find satisfaction even in the base, for that satisfaction is for ever less than desire. Can there remain for the soul in this condition anything but the retribution of eternal and immutable law? Again Tennyson's solution is a second chance *after death*.

> At last I heard a voice upon the slope
>   Cry to the summit, ' Is there any hope ? '
> To which an answer pealed from that high land,
>   But in a tongue no man could understand ;
> And on the glimmering limit far withdrawn
>   God made Himself an awful rose of dawn.

The unsatisfactory parting between King Arthur and Guinevere is patched up with the idea of immortality :

> Hereafter in that world where all are pure
> We two may meet before high God, and thou
> Wilt spring to me, and claim me thine, and know
> I am thine husband.

The answer of the Ancient Sage, if summarized, amounts to this,

> My son, the world is dark with griefs and graves,
> So dark that men cry out against the Heavens.
> Who knows but that the darkness is in man?
> The doors of Night may be the gates of Light.

If the problem is the seeming utter littleness of man in perspective of the immensity of the universe as but newly discovered, the answer is still found in the thought of immortality. The poet does not turn to the far more convincing argument that man, even though crushed, is in his very knowledge superior to the mindless mass which crushes him, and the logic of mere size is irrelevant. It is enough for Tennyson to say that, though man may for the instant seem of no moment in the scheme of things, yet he is immortal.

What is it all, if we all of us end but in being our own corpse
    coffins at last?
Swallowed in Vastness . . .

    .   .   .   .

Peace, let it be! for I loved him, and love him for ever: the
    dead are not dead, but alive.

Truth, justice, goodness, purity, have no value to the poet apart from immortality.

Truth, for Truth is Truth, he worship't, being true as he was
    brave;
Good, for Good is Good, he follow'd, yet he look'd beyond the
    grave.
Wiser there than you, that crowning barren Death as Lord
    of all,
Deem this over tragic drama's closing curtain is the pall!

    .   .   .   .

Gone for ever! Ever?—no—for since our dying race began,
Ever, ever, and for ever, was the leading light of man.

    .   .   .   .

Truth for Truth, and Good for Good, the Good, the True,
    the Pure, the Just,
Take the charm 'For ever' from them and they crumble
    into dust.

This we believe to be exaggeration. And a limit of exaggeration is reached in 'The Death of the Old Year.' The idea of immortality is dragged in in a manner little short of ludicrous:

> He lieth still: he doth not move:
> He will not see the dawn of day.
> *He hath no other life above.*

'In Memoriam' is another matter. This poem was born

out of a great experience in the poet's life. Here we shall find his best poetry on the subject of immortality, and therefore his most valuable philosophical thought. To this master poem we shall turn later, and analyse the whole scheme of thought contained in it.

Before doing so, however, there is a second answer which we desire to give to the question why immortality looms so largely in the poet's thought. It is that Tennyson had an abnormal and morbid fear of death, and a fear concerning the life after death ; a doubt— to stifle which he had to exert all his powers—that perhaps after all death might be the end. The glory of ' In Memoriam ' is that at last he comes through his fears a conqueror. He can look beyond death with quiet confidence. He had slain the demon of doubt which assailed him for many years.

But it must not be overlooked that Tennyson fought like a frightened, drowning man for a faith big enough to overcome his doubts and fears ; a faith which he felt was the only means of keeping his head above water. He seems to be arguing, at least subconsciously, ' If I am wrong, all is lost ' ; yet the strength of his fear and doubt is seen in the fact that when his feeling is unfettered he makes out a more convincing case for doubt than for faith.

From the beginning—from the ' Confessions ' of the 1830 volume, perhaps we should say—he seems to be oppressed by his own fears and doubts. He longs for the days before he was so tormented :

> Thrice happy state again to be
> The trustful infant on the knee ;
> Who lets his waxen fingers play
> About his mother's neck, and knows
> Nothing beyond his mother's eyes.
> . . . . . .
> He hath no thought of coming woes ;
> He hath no care of life and death.

There is something piteous in the prayer that ends this poem—

> Let ... Thy love
> Enlighten me. Oh, teach me yet
> Somewhat before the heavy clod
> Weighs on me, and the busy fret
> Of that sharp-headed worm begins
> In the gross blackness underneath.
>
> O weary life! O weary death!
> O spirit and heart made desolate!
> O damned vacillating state!

Nor does he find escape, we think, from this state in any complete sense until he has written the last line of 'Crossing the Bar.'

The idea of immortality looms large, then, because Tennyson felt that to reiterate the beliefs which he would dearly like to accept might make them acceptable: a pathetic and impossible procedure. Moreover, he thought the world ought to accept these beliefs also, and sometimes the lyrical is subordinated to the didactic, which is a tragedy; for what Tennyson could *feel* is of far greater moment than anything Tennyson could *think*. And, what is more, the poetry of Tennyson when he is in the grip of a kind of nameless terror, when he finds doubts and fears concerning death surging through his breast, when he is whimpering and frightened, lonely and wistful, hiding behind the faith which he was so sure ought to protect him and which did not, when he is terrified at the prospect of death and an unknown terror beyond, is to be preferred to the writings of the stately Victorian, the darling of a nation, the friend of queens, princes, and statesmen, who walked with stately tread the shaded gravel paths of Farringford and Aldworth.

We pass now to a detailed study of 'In Memoriam.' The facts concerning its origin are too well known to need more than a brief mention here. Arthur Hallam, son of Henry Hallam the historian was a brilliant youth some eighteen months younger than Tennyson, and his closest friend at Cambridge. Some critics of the poem imply that Tennyson overstates the abilities of Hallam; but his college friends all placed him far above his contemporaries, including Gladstone, as one likely to justify great and lofty expectations. Gladstone himself praised Hallam in the most glowing terms, saying that 'among his contemporaries at Eton he stood supreme,' and that he 'resembled a passing emanation from some other and less darkly chequered world.' Hallam was engaged to Tennyson's sister Emily. He left the University to read for the Bar, and lived in London with his father at 67 Wimpole Street until he accompanied the latter on a tour to the Continent. While they were staying at Vienna, Hallam died suddenly of apoplexy on September 15, 1833. The body was brought by sea to Trieste, and buried at Clevedon, on the Bristol Channel, on January 3, 1834. Tennyson, stricken with grief, wrote over a period of sixteen years the various sections of what is now called 'In Memoriam,' and later arranged them as one poem, the Prologue being written last, in 1849, and the whole published anonymously in 1850. The metre is unusual. Tennyson at first thought himself the originator of it, but it was pointed out to him that Ben Jonson and Sir Philip Sidney had both used it before him. He meant to call it 'Fragments of an Elegy'; but, though it is not one poem, as 'Adonais' or 'Lycidas' are units, though each section is itself a poem, yet at the same time the whole is a unit, as beads may each be units and yet, when threaded, form a necklace, a fairer unit still.

We shall not examine the poem stanza by stanza and line by line. This has been done once for all by A. C. Bradley in his *Commentary*. We shall rather attempt what will be more to our purpose, and, moreover, what we have never seen attempted before—

namely, to gather up the whole of the theological ideas concerning the life after death which there are in the poem, include in our survey similar ideas in other poems, and arrange these ideas into a classification; asking ourselves whether that scheme, when completed, forms a conception consistent with itself and with that projection of Christian thought which the theologian must allow to the poet.

Since the poem was written in the way we have suggested, we shall not expect to find a gradual development of ideas. In fact, it may safely be stated that there is only the most general development discernible, which may be described as a development from the darkness which falls upon the spirit at the death of a friend to the sunlight of an assurance that there is a fuller life beyond. But the graph of the poet's faith and hope does not steadily rise. Certainty, for instance, in Section xxx. is followed by a 'doubtful gleam of solace' in xxxviii. In xxx. he feels that there is 'one mute Shadow watching all'; but in xl. he grieves that, unlike the bride who goes and may return again, the dead never return; and in xc. and xci. he is longing for the sense of presence. Elements of doubt are found repeatedly right through the poem,[1] but we may say that the poet

> fought his doubts and gather'd strength,
> He would not make his judgement blind,
> He faced the spectres of the mind
> And laid them: thus he came at length
> To find a stronger faith his own.

The following classification might be used to examine any scheme of the life after death. It will be useful in gathering the ideas in the poem together for examination.

[1] Note elements of doubt in iii. 5; xii. 13; xxxviii. 8; xl.; cvii. 20; cxviii. 5; cxx. 1; cxxxi. 86–7.

A

The Fact of a Life after Death

As we should expect, the poet does not come to the acceptance of the fact of immortality by the method of the syllogism. Logical proof is not the business of poetry.

> Her care is not to part and prove.
> (xlviii.)

The fact is a fact of truth, and it breaks in on the poet through the door of feeling or emotion. As the Ancient Sage tells us,

> Thou canst not prove thou art immortal;

and, as Tennyson says in the poem we are considering,

> We have but faith: we cannot know;
> For knowledge is of things we see;
> And yet we trust it comes from thee,
> A beam in darkness: let it grow.
> (Prologue.)

Of Hallam he says,

> I *trust* he lives in Thee;

and, though that trust may become so strong as to be a moral certainty, there is no proof of immortality, and, technically, trust is as far as any one may go. Only thus, by faith and trust, can we reach

> The truths that never can be proved
> Until we close with all we loved,
> And all we flow from, soul in soul.
> (cxxxi.)

A fact reached through the emotions is not, Tennyson

says, to be any more suspected than one reached through toiling reason.

> If e'er when faith had fall'n asleep,
>   I heard a voice, ' believe no more,'
>   And heard an ever-breaking shore
> That tumbled in the Godless deep :
>
> A warmth within the breast would melt
>   The freezing reason's colder part,
>   And like a man in wrath the heart
> Stood up and answered, ' I have felt.'
>
> (cxxiv.)

Yet when all this has been said about faith it is legitimate for a poet to draw together those intimations of immortality which are part of the experience of life. This Tennyson does.

(1) The first is the character of God as the poet conceives it :

> Thou wilt not leave us in the dust ;
>   Thou madest man, he knows not why,
>   He thinks he was not made to die ;
> And Thou hast made him : Thou art just.
>
> (Prologue.)

And again in xxxiv. :

> What then were God to such as I ?
>   'Twere hardly worth my while to choose
>   Of things all mortal, or to use
> A little patience ere I die ;
>
> 'Twere best at once to sink to peace,
>   Like birds the charming serpent draws,
>   To drop head-foremost in the jaws
> Of vacant darkness and to cease.

(2) The second is the character of man :

> And he, shall he,
>
> Man, her last work, who seem'd so fair,
>   Such splendid purpose in his eyes,
>   Who roll'd the psalm to wintry skies,
> Who built him fanes of fruitless prayer,

> Who trusted God was love indeed
> And love Creation's final law—
> Tho' Nature, red in tooth and claw
> With ravine, shriek'd against his creed—
>
> Who loved, who suffer'd countless ills,
> Who battled for the True, the Just,
> Be blown about the desert dust,
> Or seal'd within the iron hills?
>
> No more? A monster then, a dream,
> A discord. Dragons of the prime,
> That tare each other in their slime,
> Were mellow music match'd with him.
>   (lvi.)

The poet feels that there is an intimation of immortality in what he calls on two occasions 'our mystic frame.'

> My own dim life should teach me this,
> That life shall live for evermore,
> Else earth is darkness at the core,
> And dust and ashes all that is.

With this we may perhaps quote a passage from 'The Ring,' in which the poet speaks of catching a glimpse of the eternal life, for which he thinks man destined, in the flash of a woman's eyes:

> And there the light of other life, which lives
> Beyond our burial and our buried eyes,
> Gleam'd for a moment in her own on earth.

In section xiv. we have the same kind of intimation, where the poet cannot accept the thought that anything so splendid as the personality of Hallam can have passed into nothingness. So also in 'The Two Voices':

> A still small voice spake unto me,
> 'Thou art so full of misery,
> Were it not better not to be?'
>
> Then to the still small voice I said;
> 'Let me not cast in endless shade
> What is so wonderfully made.'

And in ' Love and Duty ' the poet asks what he feels is an unanswerable question :

> And only he, this wonder, dead, become
> Mere highway dust?

Human life frequently, and especially in the case of Hallam, is so incomplete that another life seems demanded. As he contemplates unfinished courses he cries,
> so much to do,
> So little done, such things to be,
> How know I what had need of thee,
> For thou wert strong as thou wert true ?
> (lxxiii.)

(3) A third intimation confirmatory of the fact of the life after death is man's own longing for it, not only on his own account, but on that of his friends :

> Thy creature whom I found so fair,
> I trust he lives in Thee, and there
> I find him worthier to be loved.

And though this longing is not universal, as some thinkers have supposed, it is sufficiently widespread almost to justify the adjective, for

> Whatever crazy sorrow saith,
> No life that lives with human breath
> Has ever truly long'd for death.

> 'Tis life, whereof our nerves are scant,
> Oh, life, not death, for which we pant ;
> More life, and fuller, that I want.

And so the poet has no quarrel with death, for it is the gateway to a fairer life :

> I wage not any feud with Death,
> For changes wrought on form and face,
> No lower life that earth's embrace
> May breed with him, can fright my faith.

> Eternal process moving on,
>   From state to state the spirit walks;
>   And these are but the shatter'd stalks
> Or ruined chrysalis of one.
>
> (lxxxii.)

Men need not fear death. Life, the poet says in the 'Holy Grail,' is 'our dull side of death'; and in a very beautiful figure in 'Lancelot and Elaine' he tells us that death is

> like a friend's voice from a distant field,
> Approaching through the darkness.

B

The Nature of a Life after Death

(1) The life after death, in Tennyson's views is to be a continuation of personal and self-conscious existence. It is not to be absorption into the Infinite, or what the poet calls the 'general soul.' He says in xlvii.,

> That each, who seems a separate whole,
>   Should move his rounds, and fusing all
>   The skirts of self again, should fall
> Remerging in the general soul,
>
> In faith as vague as all unsweet:
>   Eternal form shall still divide
>   The eternal soul from all beside;
> And I shall know him when we meet.

Details of this form the poet does not discern. He says (lxx.) :

> I cannot see the features right,
>   When on the gloom I strive to paint
>   The face I know; the hues are faint,
> And mix with hollow masks of night.

It is interesting to notice that Tennyson rejects the materialistic conception of the resurrection of the body after death, though that conception was part of the orthodox theological thought of his day. At death, he feels, the body is done with. It passes into the soil and becomes part of it, and is absorbed into other forms of life :

> And from his ashes may be made
> The violet of his native land.
> (xviii.)

At the same time it seems to him a 'fearful thing' that the Hallam he knew should have become pure spirit. The conception is

> An awful thought, a life removed,
> The human-hearted man I loved,
> A Spirit, not a breathing voice.
> (xiii.)

It is so difficult to accept the conception of a friend's translation to a purely spiritual existence and yet feel that one has not lost something, in losing the familiar form, the sound of the voice, the grasp of the hand. So at times the poet would restore the friend, if he could, to corporeal life again :

> if this might be,
> I, falling on his faithful heart,
> Would, breathing thro' his lips, impart
> The life that almost dies in me.

Such a desire finds its supreme expression in the famous lines beginning, ' Break, break, break '—

> But O for the touch of a vanish'd hand,
> And the sound of a voice that is still!

(2) The nature of the life after death, as Tennyson conceives it, allows the possibility, and indeed affirms the actuality, of reunion with, and recognition of, the friend he has lost. He speaks of

> My Arthur, whom I shall not see
> Till all my widow'd race be run.
> (ix.)

He recognizes the possibility of a long sleep immediately following death (xliii.) He felt that there may be a further separation as each passes to a different sphere of activity (xlvii.) ; but, at any rate, he and his friend will meet and enjoy one another's society, and the word 'endless,' which he uses in this connexion, seems to defer the possible separation to some very remote time :

> And we shall sit at endless feast
> Enjoying each the other's good.

It is necessarily implied, of course, if the idea of reunion and recognition be held, that the soul will remember the life on earth when it has passed ' beyond these voices.' This the poet makes clear in xlv. He points out that if the soul in the next life has forgotten the earth-life it will be unable to recognize itself. It would have to re-acquire the consciousness of individuality and identity, and in this case what, in the perspective of eternity, is the significance of this life ?

There are other references, outside ' In Memoriam,' to the thought of the meeting after death of the friends we know here. Says Enoch Arden, in a passage of deep pathos :

> And now there is but one of all my blood
> Who will embrace me in the world-to-be.

Balan greets Balin, as they lie a-dying, with the words :

> Good night, true brother, here ! good morrow there !

King Arthur parts with Guinevere with the words :

> Hereafter, in that world where all are pure
> We two may meet before high God, and thou
> Wilt spring to me, and claim me thine, and know
> I am thine husband—not a smaller soul,
> Nor Lancelot, nor another. Leave me that,
> I charge thee, my last hope.

And Guinevere hopes to

> be his mate hereafter in the heavens.

C

The Conditions of Life Beyond the Grave

When we come to ask what the poet paints into his picture of conditions beyond the grave, we find that he says nothing of hell and little of heaven. Tennyson found it impossible to accept the current orthodoxy of his day on the subject of hell. We are told in the *Memoir* that his son made some reference to it when reading aloud to his father in 1889. The poet said bluntly, ' That is eternal hell which I do not believe.'[1] One day towards the end of his life he made Hallam look into the Revised Version to see how the translators had interpreted the word αἰώνιος, and was very much disappointed to find that the word ' everlasting ' had been used instead of a word he uses himself, 'aeonian';[2] for ' he never would believe that Christ could preach everlasting punishment.'[3]

The only references Tennyson makes in his poetry to the conception of hell current in his day are made in poems other than ' In Memoriam.' In ' Guinevere ' we find a passing reference of little moment to

> the Powers that tend the soul,
> To help it from the death that cannot die ;

and again, concerning Lancelot,

> Pray for him that he 'scape the doom of fire.

---

[1] *Memoir*, vol. i., p. 715.
[2] e.g.   ' Draw down aeonian hills, and sow
            The dust of continents to be.'
[3] When Aubrey de Vere was giving his views on eternal punishment, Tennyson tried to laugh him away from the subject, and suggested that eternal punishment for himself would probably be to be forced to listen to ' Huxley and Tyndall disputing eternally on the non-existence of God.'

In 'Despair' we find the lines :

We broke away from the Christ, our human brother and friend,
For He spake, or it seem'd that He spake, of a hell without help, without end.

These are the only references to hell in Tennyson's poetry, and they are all insignificant.

Heaven means to the poet spiritual progress and service. We can classify both these ideas under the general idea of heaven.

Progress, growth, and development for the soul after death are assumed. We note in the passage quoted above—

in that world *where all are pure*,

and the line in 'In Memoriam '—

there
I find him *worthier to be loved*.
(Prologue.)

Section lxxxii. implies the same idea :

Eternal process moving on,
From state to state the spirit walks.

Hallam is conceived as exerting his quickened powers in some kind of heavenly service :

And, doubtless unto thee is given
A life that bears immortal fruit
In those great offices that suit
The full-grown energies of heaven ;
(xl.)

and this idea is the most prominent in the poet's idea of heaven. He never dwells on the thought of rest in the world to be. The line,

Where the wicked cease from troubling and the weary are at rest,

expresses an exceptional thought. Tennyson, in every other passage, describes the condition of the soul in the other world as one of activity. So in 'Wages,' Virtue

> desires no isles of the blest, no quiet seats of the just,
> To rest in a golden grove, or to bask in summer sky:
> Give her the wages of going on, and not to die.

Sir John Franklin is pictured, in the lines written for his cenotaph in Westminster Abbey, as still engaged on the work of exploration to which he gave his life :

> Not here! the white North has thy bones; and thou,
>   Heroic sailor soul,
> Art passing on thine happier voyage now
>   Towards no earthly pole.

And of the Duke of Wellington, in the famous ode, the poet says,

> There must be other nobler work to do
> Than when he fought at Waterloo—

a sentiment which, perhaps, savours of the use of immortality as a panacea for ills not understood.

Progress and service are the two words which summarize Tennyson's conception of the condition of the soul after death. It is a worthy conception, both in its content and in its restraint :

> No sudden heaven, nor sudden hell, for man,
> But thro' the will of One who knows and rules—
> And utter knowledge is but utter love—
> Aeonian Evolution, swift or slow,
> Thro' all the Spheres—an ever-opening height,
> An ever lessening earth.

D

THE CONSUMMATION OF THE LIFE AFTER DEATH

Our next classification naturally asks what is the goal to which this progress is all tending—that is, if there be such a goal in the thought of the poet. What is the mighty cause in which this service is being rendered?

HP

There seems to be ever in the poet's mind a climax to the process begun here and continued after death. His mind, we think, keeps a central place for

> one far-off divine event,
> To which the whole creation moves;
> (cxxxi.)

though he leaves us sharing his own doubt concerning the nature of that event. Many of the poet's expressions seem to suggest a further life in other worlds, and the soul passing from embodiment to embodiment upon them. 'From orb to orb, from veil to veil,' 'through all the spheres,' 'from state to state,' 'thy vain worlds'—these phrases suggest this idea. Even the reunion with Hallam may, after a time, be broken by the latter passing of necessity to further spheres:

> He seeks at least
> Upon the last and sharpest height,
> Before the spirits fade away,
> Some landing-place, to clasp and say
> 'Farewell! We lose ourselves in light!'
> (xlvii.)

If we might hazard a speculation as to the nature of that divine event which is to mark the consummation of the after-life, we would suggest that it means the gathering in, after a purifying process, of all souls, and the completion of the long history of the perfecting of the spirit of man. This is what the theologian calls the theory of universalism. Tennyson, if we accept 'In Memoriam' as containing his views, as he told us to do, definitely accepts this position, basing it on the element of divinity in man:

> Oh yet we trust that somehow good
> Will be the final goal of ill,
> To pangs of nature, sins of will,
> Defects of doubt, and taints of blood;

> That nothing walks with aimless feet;
> That not one life shall be destroy'd
> Or cast as rubbish to the void,
> When God hath made the pile complete;
>
> . . . .
>
> Behold, we know not anything;
> I can but trust that good shall fall
> At last—far off—*at last*, to all,
> And every winter change to spring.
> (liv.)

And, as we have said, this wish is based on the divinity of humanity:

> The wish, that of the living whole
> No life may fail beyond the grave,
> Derives it not from what we have
> The likest God within the soul?
> (lv.)

Doubts assail him, for nature, at any rate, seems 'careless of the single life'; and the poet falters, but rests in the *hope* that the whole race, possibly after purging suffering, will at last emerge purified and entire:

> I falter where I firmly trod,
> And falling with my weight of cares
> Upon the great world's altar-stairs
> That slope thro' darkness up to God,
>
> I stretch lame hands of faith, and grope,
> And gather dust and chaff, and call
> To what I feel is Lord of all,
> And faintly trust the larger hope.
> (lv.)

We have the same idea in the closing lines of the 'Vision of Sin':

> At last I heard a voice upon the slope
> Cry to the summit, 'Is there any hope?'
> To which an answer peal'd from that high land,
> But in a tongue no man could understand;
> And on the glimmering limit far withdrawn
> God made Himself an awful rose of Dawn.

In the closing lines of ' The Progress of Spring ' we have the same thought :

> And men have hopes, which race the restless blood,
>   That after many changes may succeed
> Life, which is life indeed ;

and in ' The Making of Man ' :

Man as yet is being made, and ere the crowning Age of ages,
Shall not aeon after aeon pass and touch him into shape?

All about him shadow still, but, while the races flower and fade,
Prophet-eyes may catch a glory slowly gaining on the shade,
Till the peoples all are one, and all their voices blend in choric
Hallelujah to the Maker ' It is finish'd. Man is made.'

E

COMMUNION BETWEEN THE LIVING AND THE DEAD

The human desire to peer through the veil of death finds expression in Tennyson's poetry. We have, for instance, the exquisite lyric, ' O that 'twere possible,' containing the lines,

> Ah, Christ, that it were possible
>   For one short hour to see
> The souls we loved, that they might tell us
>   What and where they be ;

and it is interesting to notice that, although doubts often assail him, the poet does believe the dead to be very near those whom they loved on earth.

On the first Christmas after Hallam's death, as they weave the holly round the Christmas hearth, and make ' vain pretence of gladness,' it is

> with an awful sense
> Of one mute Shadow watching all ;
>   (xxx.)

and the feeling that the dead are silent watchers of earth's activities is expressed again in lxiii., beginning,

> So may'st thou watch me where I weep.

It is also expressed in the ode on the Great Duke, and the 'May Queen.' Though the poet speaks of it as an 'awful sense,' yet in another mood he desires the sense of the presence of the dead and prays to receive it. A very beautiful section expresses this longing, beginning,

> Be near me when my light is low,
>   When the blood creeps, and the nerves prick
> And tingle; and the heart is sick,
> And all the wheels of Being slow.
>   (l.)

And this desire holds even though another question arises:

> Do wé indeed desire the dead
>   Should still be near us at our side?
>   Is there no baseness we would hide?
> No inner vileness that we dread?
>   (li.)

for the experience of the sense of nearness will be one that is profitable and helpful, since

> There must be wisdom with great Death:
>   The dead shall look me thro' and thro';
>   ' (li.)

for

> Ye watch, like God, the rolling hours
>   With larger other eyes than ours,
> To make allowance for us all.

A question of intense interest is whether the spirits of the dead, even if near, can communicate with those who are still living the earth life, and vice versa. The poet's answer would seem to be that if the word 'communion' be used instead of the word 'communication,' there is a link between souls on this side of the grave and those on the other. The poet says:

> I watch thee from the quiet shore;
>   Thy spirit up to mine can reach;
> But in dear words of human speech
> We two *communicate* no more.
>   (lxxxv.)

118 THE AFTER-WORLD OF THE POETS

In section xciii. the poet dismisses the idea that the dead ever make their presence known by any vision of themselves to the outward eye; but feels that the sense of presence can be realized most fully when all the faculties are quiescent, when, in a spirit of loving meditation on the dead, the human spirit leans out of the window of that prison-house the body:

> In vain shalt thou, or any, call
>   The spirits from their golden day,
>   Except, like them, thou too canst say,
> My spirit is at peace with all.
>
> They haunt the silence of the breast,
>   Imaginations calm and fair,
>   The memory like a cloudless air,
> The conscience as a sea at rest:
>
> But when the heart is full of din,
>   And doubt beside the portal waits,
>   They can but listen at the gates,
> And hear the household jar within.
>   (xciv.)

Yet no vision of the dead is expected:

> I shall not see thee. Dare I say
>   No spirit ever brake the band
>   That stays him from the native land
> Where first he walk'd when claspt in clay?
>   (xciii.)

The experience will be superior to the vision of a ghost. Its richness will be in the calm sense of the presence of the loved one himself:

> No visual shade of someone lost,
>   But he, the Spirit himself, may come
>   Where all the nerve of sense is numb;
> Spirit to Spirit, Ghost to Ghost.
>   (xciii.)

The poet pleads for this communion, this sense of presence:

> O, therefore from thy sightless range[1]
> With gods in unconjectured bliss,
> O, from the distance of the abyss
> Of tenfold-complicated change,
>
> Descend, and touch, and enter; hear
> The wish too strong for words to name;
> That in this blindness of the frame
> My Ghost may feel that thine is near.

Section xcv. one is tempted to quote in full. In beautiful language it gives us a description of the poet's supreme experience of the nearness of his friend. The scene is the beloved garden at Somersby in which the evening meal has been served. In the quiet twilight of the summer evening, after the meal is over, the poet and his friends sing old favourite songs together. Then gradually the night falls,

> the trees
> Laid their dark arms about the field.

The others leave the poet alone in the garden and retire to rest. Light after light goes out in the house, accentuating the sense of loneliness. He reads over again some of the letters of the dead friend. 'The silent speaking words' of the letter have a strange effect on him, and a climax is reached when the poet feels that Hallam is *there*.

> So word by word, and line by line,
> The dead man touch'd me from the past,
> And all at once it seem'd at last
> The living soul was flash'd on mine.

It is a wonderful experience. The poet, during its

[1] 'the place where thou rangest invisible' (A. C. Bradley).

course, seems to catch a vision of ultimate reality; seems to see law, meaning, and order in what at other times has appeared unintelligible. Then the 'trance' ends, 'stricken thro' with doubt,' leaving behind an uncertainty as to whether it was veridical; but the impression of it remains in the mind, and the poet cannot find words which adequately express his experience.

In the last four stanzas of the section he describes the passing of the trance in language which Professor Bradley calls 'one of the most wonderful descriptive passages in all poetry . . . the breeze seeming to recall the coming and passing of the wind of the spirit in the trance, and the mingling of the dim lights of east and west being seen as that meeting of life and death which had just been experienced as the precursor of an endless union to come.'[1]

Probably the poet is referring to this same trance in cxxii. :

> Oh, wast thou with me, dearest, then?

and he craves a repetition of the experience :

> If thou wert with me, and the grave
> Divide us not, be with me now,
> And enter in at breast and brow,
> Till all my blood, a fuller wave,
>
> Be quicken'd with a livelier breath.

The same thought of a kind of spiritual communion without words or vision seems to be suggested in less beautiful language in 'The May Queen' :

If I can I'll come again, mother, from out my resting-place;
Tho' you'll not see me, mother, I shall look upon your face;
Tho' I cannot speak a word, I shall hearken what you say,
And be often, often with you when you think I'm far away.

[1] *Commentary on 'In Memoriam,'* pp. 191–2.

Tennyson, it seems to the writer, gathered the grain in spiritualism and cast the chaff away. To him communion seemed higher, deeper, closer than communication. The latter seemed to degrade the former, because it flung out no challenge to the higher powers of perception, faith, and love. The former seemed to be above the necessity of the latter. He was repelled by the paraphernalia of spiritualism. 'I am convinced,' he said,[1] 'that God and the ghosts of men would choose something other than table-legs through which to speak to the heart of man.' Yet the dead were often near, and were even able to share, through sympathy, in the experiences of the living:

> Can clouds of nature stain
>   The starry clearness of the free?
>   How is it? Canst thou feel for me
> Some painless sympathy with pain?
>   (lxxxv.)

And the answer is in the affirmative, since those on the other side have a far-off glimpse of the 'serene result of all' earth's striving.

The above arrangement gives us a convenient way of surveying Tennyson's conception of an after-world. Every reference to it in the whole of Tennyson's work is included in this chapter, and a careful study of the passages shows that the scheme is consistent with itself. By this is meant that it does not take up in one regard a position which is denied or contradicted in another. The main features of the scheme are found of course in ' In Memoriam,' and we have the poet's own authority for concluding that the scheme in ' In Memoriam ' represents his own faith.

We have made two criticisms of the scheme in speaking of the reasons for the prominence of immortality in Tennyson's thought. We wish to advance one

[1] *Memoir*, p. 705.

other criticism of a different kind. It is that all the main positions taken up in modern theology with regard to the subject of eschatology may be found in 'In Memoriam,' written three quarters of a century ago. Theology is slowly, by a very different route, creeping towards the heights to which the poets soared in the nineteenth century. It is an impressive fact that from the sources of poetic insight and feeling a poet is found expressing ideas for which the theologian would almost be burned at the stake, and yet ideas which the theologian is found substantiating, somewhat hesitantly, fifty years later. It is a fact which points to the conclusion that poets—especially in matters of speculation like the one we have been considering—are the truest teachers of their generation, the 'hierophants of an unapprehended inspiration,' the 'mirrors of the gigantic shadows which futurity casts upon the present.' They dream the dreams of the world of to-morrow. They lift men's eyes to wide horizons. They send men out from their presence with hearts encouraged and ennobled, with faces turned towards the dawn and eyes uplifted to the hills.

IV

THE CONTRIBUTION OF DOUBT

(Arnold, Clough, and Swinburne)

IV
THE CONTRIBUTION OF DOUBT

In tracing the idea of immortality through the poetry of the nineteenth century, we must be careful not to limit our inquiry to those poets who believed in it. The doubts of the poets form a contribution worthy of very careful consideration. We use the word 'doubt' in its widest possible connotation. If a poet posits the idea of immortality in a number of poems, and is sceptical about it in a number of other poems which, from the point of view of poetry, are equally worthy of consideration, then we should rank him with the poets of doubt as far as this subject is concerned. Tennyson, for instance, had his doubts, but he was never sceptical about immortality. We use the word 'doubt' also in its strongest sense. If a poet only accepts the idea of immortality in a number of minor poems, and denies it in his best work, we have a case of doubt which amounts to denial. We use the word here to connote every degree of doubt, from inconsistency to denial. In Arnold, Clough, and Swinburne we have a gradually increasing doubt which, as we shall see, reaches virtual denial in Swinburne.

I

Matthew Arnold (1822–1888)

To make a consistent scheme of the religious ideas of Matthew Arnold is an impossibility. We find that, concerning any religious ideas upon which he touched, he says things which contradict one another. There is one clue which takes us a little way. We are faced by the two completely different ways of arriving at a judgement which we noted in the first chapter. We have Arnold the poet and Arnold the essayist. We have the apprehension of the former and the opinions of the latter. We have the artist who can write the following lines to a cuckoo departing with the bloom of early spring:

> Too quick despairer, wherefore wilt thou go?
> Soon will the high Midsummer pomps come on,
> Soon will the musk carnations break and swell,
> Soon shall we have gold-dusted snapdragon,
> Sweet-William with his homely cottage-smell,
> And stocks in fragrant blow;
> Roses that down the alleys shine afar,
> And open, jasmine-muffled lattices,
> And groups under the dreaming garden-trees,
> And the full moon, and the white evening-star.[1]

We have also the academic Inspector of Schools, with some rather death-ridden theological theories and with a great passion to do battle with various bishops who 'desire to say a word for the doctrine of the Godhead of the Eternal Son.'

This clue leads us a little way. I think it explains Arnold's apparent self-distrust in his own poetry. For he does seem, instead of letting himself go, to pull himself up in his verse, as one who says, 'This will never do. Reason is against it.' Whereas in his prose he does not restrain himself. One might almost say that he better reveals the mood of the true poet when he is writing prose, and vice versa. The two phases do not retain a sufficient distinction in their operation in Arnold. He is often illogical in his prose, and uses cold reason in his verse. We have a lack of restraint in some essays which we would dearly love to see in some poems, which are almost too careful, too restrained, too 'cultured.'

But the clue of the fundamental division which

[1] 'Thyrsis.'

should separate poet from essayist does not account for the inconsistent thinking in either poems or essays; for if we take each separately we shall find Arnold taking up positions which are irreconcilable, and doing so in the most casual and dogmatic manner.[1]

Mr. Herbert Paul, in his book on the poet, tells us that Mr. Frederic Harrison ' sought vainly in him a system of philosophy with principles coherent, interdependent, subordinate, and derivative '; and Mr. Gladstone said that Matthew Arnold ' combined a sincere devotion to the Christian religion with a faculty for presenting it in such a form as to be recognizable neither by friend nor foe.' Take only one illustration, in passing, of this lack of consistency and this vagueness of religious thought. In one of his essays Arnold tells us that we may set aside the idea that the God of this universe is a person as one that is ' unprofitable and mischievous.' God, to him, is ' a stream of tendency by which all things strive to fulfil the law of their being,' or ' the enduring power not ourselves which makes for righteousness.' So, in translating the Old Testament, he uses the expression ' The Eternal ' for God, to which, it is interesting to note, Professor Moffatt returns in his recent translation of the Old Testament. Yet again and again, in prose and poetry, Arnold uses the word God in a personal sense, and this, not when putting words into the mouths of dramatic characters, but in poems which would certainly seem to express his own views. In the poem ' Farewell' he refers to God as ' the eternal Father,' and as ' Father ' in ' Rugby Chapel.'

The present writer believes that Matthew Arnold's religion can best be understood by saying that he is both stoic and humanitarian at the same time, and, further, that his humanitarianism is strongly flavoured

[1] An unpleasant confirmation of this dogmatism is seen in his answer to his sister, who once complained to him that he ' was becoming as dogmatic as Ruskin ': ' Yes,' replied the literary critic, turned amateur theologian, ' but Ruskin was dogmatic and wrong.'

with the Christian spirit. Let us consider this statement. Stoicism, popularly interpreted, makes a great appeal to a nature like Arnold's. It calls for moral endurance. It stands for unflinching courage in facing either inward or outward evil. It will have no cushions of comfort on which to fall back in time of trouble. It stakes all on the position accepted by the intellect as rational, and will not allow emotion to sweep it away from that anchorage which it regards as the only anchorage of the soul. So of Arnold himself we might say :

> he, within,
> Took measure of his soul and knew its strength,
> And by that silent knowledge, day by day,
> Was calm'd, ennobled, comforted, sustained.
>
> ('Mycerinus.')

' No one,' he says in a letter dated March 3, 1865, ' has a stronger and more abiding sense than I have of the " daemonic element "—as Goethe called it—which underlies and encompasses our life ; but I think, as Goethe thought, that the right thing is, while conscious of this element and of all that there is inexplicable round one, to keep pushing on one's posts into the darkness, and to establish no post that is not perfectly in light and firm. One gains nothing in the darkness by being, like Shelley, as incoherent as the darkness itself.' And this is Arnold's position in all things.

Nor will he warm his heart, even in moments of great personal sorrow, at any more emotional fire. At Harrow—whither he had gone to live for the better education of his children—on November 23, 1867, his eldest son, Thomas, who had always been an invalid, died. Mr. G. W. E. Russell called on the poet the next morning, ' and,' Mr. Russell says, ' the author with whom he was consoling himself was Marcus Aurelius.' And a passage in *Essays on Criticism* tells us what Arnold thought of the philosopher. ' He was perhaps the most beautiful figure in history. He is one of those consoling and hope-inspiring marks which stand for ever to remind our weak and easily discouraged race how high human goodness and perseverance have once been carried, and may be carried again.'

In spite of Arnold's stoicism, however, a deep humanitarianism continually breaks in and makes him more human, and therefore more lovable. He becomes, because of it, better than his creed. It seems as if he did his best to satisfy his hungry spirit on the husks of pure rationalism, and yet stole away at times to feed on the more satisfying, more appetizing, but self-forbidden fruits of a less exacting philosophy. A certain letter illustrates this, and at the same time keeps us near to the subject of immortality. Writing to his sister Fanny on the death of his youngest son, Basil, who died on January 4, 1868, he says: ' And so this loss comes to me just after my forty-fifth birthday, with so much other " suffering in the flesh "—the departure of youth, cares of many kinds, an almost painful anxiety about public matters—to remind us *that the time past of our life may suffice us*, words which have haunted me for the past year or two, and that " we should no longer live the rest of our time in the flesh to the lusts of men but to the will of God." However different the interpretation we put on much of the facts and history of Christianity, we may unite in the bonds of this call, which is true for all of us, and for me, above all, how full of meaning and warning.'

Consider the warm devotional sympathy with which he speaks, in *Literature and Dogma*, of the poetry of the Old Testament and its sublime message of righteousness! Consider the almost wistful regard for the ' secret of Jesus ' and the ' method of Jesus'! Consider the passion to understand the mind of St. Paul by one who does not believe with his mind in the personality of God! If we found a label for his religion at all, we should feel desirous of borrowing one of his own phrases and altering it. We should label his religion

'Marcus-Aurelian morality touched by Christian—or at least by deeply humanitarian—emotion.'

In a sense, like every true poet, Matthew Arnold mirrors the mental ferment of his age. And this was a time when the scientific aspect of every kind of problem was being emphasized and the scientific method of approach most in public favour. The ideas of 'miracle,' of the 'prophecy' of events in the far-distant future, of 'revelation,' and of 'inspiration' in any sense different from that common to all great literature, were being scrutinized in the light of the 'high white star of Truth,' where previously they had been taken for granted by an uncritical and wonder-loving people. German professors had long been busy with both the Old and the New Testaments, and at last their findings were beginning to percolate to the mind of the lay reader, with results disastrous or illuminating according to the capacity of that mind to accept new truth. Obedient to this new spirit of the age, Arnold tried to open out a new world of Christian thinking with all excrescences pruned away. But, though the old world became uninhabitable for Arnold and for many another, yet the new was never a reality, either for him or for his contemporaries. As he says in the well-known 'Stanzas from the Grande Chartreuse,' he wandered between two worlds.

> For rigorous teachers seized my youth,
> And purged its faith, and trimm'd its fire,
> Show'd me the high, white star of Truth,
> There bade me gaze, and there aspire.
> Even now their whispers pierce the gloom:
> What dost thou in this living tomb?
>
> Forgive me, masters of the mind!
> At whose behest I long ago
> So much unlearnt, so much resign'd.
> I come not here to be your foe!
> I seek these anchorites, not in ruth
> To curse and to deny your truth;

> Not as their friend, or child, I speak!
> But as, on some far northern strand,
> Thinking of his own Gods, a Greek
> In pity and mournful awe might stand
> Before some fallen Runic stone—
> For both were faiths, and both are gone.
>
> Wandering between two worlds, one dead,
> The other powerless to be born,
> With nowhere yet to rest my head,
> Like these, on earth, I wait forlorn.

Yet, although it is true that Arnold carried the pruning process a little too far—as when he interprets the command in the Old Testament, ' Fear God and keep His commandments,' as ' Reverently obey the eternal power moving us to fulfil the true law of our being '; and the command in the New Testament, ' Watch that ye may be counted worthy to stand before the Son of Man,' as ' So live to be worthy of that high and true ideal of man and of man's life which shall be at last victorious ' [1]—yet at the same time he did very valuable work in showing the foolishness of the theory of verbal inspiration, of a fantastic theory of prophecy, and of a superstitious view of miracle; though in the last case he does not seem to realize—so the present writer thinks—that the stumbling-block to man's acceptance of a certain view of miracle is not that it is not in harmony with the laws of nature as he knows them, but that it asks him to believe that those laws are, under certain conditions, suspended or contradicted. That is to say, man's main difficulty is not in accepting the *super*natural, but the *contra*-natural; not the happenings which are above nature as we know it—these must go on occurring until our knowledge of nature is complete—but those which we are asked to believe manifest the reversion or suspension of laws by a divine Power interposing in the universe at a certain time for a certain purpose. Such

[1] *Literature and Dogma*, p. 22.

an interference would mean that God acknowledged the poverty and inefficient nature of the scheme He drew up at the beginning of all things, and that man is liable at any moment to find his knowledge confounded by a divine juggling-trick.

It is always valuable to have the point of view of a literary man on matters of practical religion. He has no axe to grind, no case to make out, no undue bias, and few theological predilections. It was in this capacity that Arnold wrote, 'not,' as he said, ' to disturb any one's faith, but to convince these who could not believe in the performance of miracles or the fulfilment of prophecies that they need not therefore become materialists.' ' Je n'ai pas parlé en théologien,' he wrote to M. Fontanes, ' mais en homme de lettres.' It is a very interesting fact to note in passing that many prophecies which Arnold himself made concerning the direction which progressive Christian thinking would take have already come true, and others seem likely to do so.

One is tempted to wonder whether these conflicts in the mind between the stoic on the one hand and the humanitarian on the other; between the teacher on the one hand and the poet on the other; between the rationalist on the one hand, whose system of religious thought seemed to him all-important, and, on the other hand, that same rationalist, disillusioned, disappointed, and crestfallen because his system was not immediately accepted by the 'masses,' did not give to his poetry that air of haunting sadness which so much of it breathes.

                        The Sea of Faith
Was once, too, at the full, and round earth's shore
Lay like the folds of a bright girdle furl'd.
But now I only hear
Its melancholy, long, withdrawing roar,
Retreating, to the breath
Of the night-wind, down the vast edges drear
And naked shingles of the world.

> the world, which seems
> To lie before us like a land of dreams,
> So various, so beautiful, so new,
> Hath really neither joy, nor love, nor light,
> Nor certitude, nor peace, nor help for pain;
> And we are here as on a darkling plain
> Swept with confused alarms of struggle and flight,
> Where ignorant armies clash by night.[1]

Professor Saintsbury[2] quotes some lines from Principal Shairp's *Balliol Scholars*, 1840–1843, published in 1873, which he thinks express the spirit of Arnold. We

> knew not then the undertone that flows,
> So calmly sad, through all his stately lay.

And constantly, when we are with Arnold,

> through the hum of torrent lone,
> And brooding mountain-bee,
> There sobs I know not what ground-tone
> Of human agony.[3]

We cannot get away from

> His sad lucidity of soul.[4]

There is, as we have said, a vagueness and lack of consistency in regard to every idea which Matthew Arnold takes up. The teacher says one thing, and, if the poet says the same, he says it less austerely. The stoic says one thing, the humanitarian something kindlier. The rationalist says one thing, the affectionate-natured, child-loving man says something more instinctive. Let us use the idea of immortality to illustrate this. Frederic Harrison so interprets the former aspects of the poet's dicta that he writes as follows: 'His intellect rejected the belief that there was even probable evidence for the celestial immortality

---

[1] 'Dover Beach.' [2] *Matthew Arnold*, p. 6.
[3] 'In Memory of the Author of "Obermann."' [4] 'Resignation.'

of the soul'; yet, rationalist though Arnold the essayist is, listen to the poet! The poem 'Farewell,' in the 'Switzerland' series, contains little more than a sheer revelling in the idea of personal and conscious immortality:

> we shall one day gain, life past,
> Clear prospect o'er our being's whole;
> Shall see ourselves, and learn at last
> Our true affinities of soul.
> . . . . .
> Then, in the eternal Father's smile,
> Our soothed, encouraged souls will dare
> To seem as free from pride and guile,
> As good, as generous as they are.

Space forbids extensive quotation, but one is sure that no one could write these kindling verses who did not himself believe in immortality.

Take another contrast, with the difference that here the prose seems kindlier than the verse: 'The region of our hopes and presentiments extends, as we have said, far beyond the region of what we can know with certainty. What we reach but by hope and presentiment may yet be true; and he would be a narrow reasoner who denied, for instance, all validity to the idea of immortality, because the idea rests on presentiment mainly, and does not admit of certain demonstration.'[1]

Turn to the poems, and we may find this written of death:

> Stern law of every mortal lot
> Which man, proud man, finds hard to bear,
> And builds himself, I know not what
> Of second life, I know not where.

Mr. R. H. Hutton,[2] quoting the above verse, seems to be blind to the conflicting views which, we have suggested, Matthew Arnold put forth in his writings. He says, 'Mr. Arnold will hear nothing of the promise

[1] *Literature and Dogma*, p. 144.
[2] *Essays on some of the Modern Guides to English Thought*, p. 125.

of immortality. That is to him *Aberglaube*, overbelief, belief in excess of evidence.' We believe that this statement is simply not true. To say that Arnold will hear nothing of the promise of immortality is to overlook the *cumulative* significance of the following quotations :

> Nor will that day dawn at a human nod,
> When, bursting through the network superposed
> By selfish occupation—plot and plan,
>
> Lust, avarice, envy—liberated man,
> All difference with his fellow-mortal closed,
> Shall be left standing face to face with God ;[1]

and again the same idea in ' The New Sirens ' :

> at God's tribunal
> Some large answer you shall hear.

We turn to ' Requiescat,' and read :

> Her cabin'd, ample spirit,
> It flutter'd and fail'd for breath.
> To-night it doth inherit
> The vasty hall of death ;

or the passage in ' A Wish,' where he speaks of

> The future and its viewless things—
> That undiscover'd mystery,

when referring to death, and thus reveals some kind of belief in something beyond, even if all that can be said about it is that it is unknown ; which, after all, is as much as any one can say with certainty.

Other passages go further. In 'Human Life' we have the idea of meeting the ' Heavenly Friend ' after the voyage of life. And in ' The Scholar Gipsy ' the poet says :

> To the just-pausing Genius we remit
> Our worn-out life, and are—what we have been.

' Thyrsis,' the beautiful elegy to his friend Arthur Hugh

[1] ' To a Republican Friend, Continued.'

Clough, who died at Florence in 1861, breathes the spirit of immortality:

> To a boon southern country he is fled,
>   And now in happier air,
> Wandering with the great Mother's train divine
> (And purer or more subtle soul than thee,
> I trow, the mighty Mother doth not see)
> Within a folding of the Apennine,
> Thou hearest the immortal chants of old!

And, as the poet cannot believe that his beloved Thyrsis has ceased to be, so he cannot believe that his own father, with that forceful personality, has passed into nothingness:

> O strong soul, by what shore
> Tarriest thou now? For that force,
> Surely, has not been left vain!
> Somewhere, surely, afar,
> In the sounding labour-house vast
> Of being, is practised that strength,
> Zealous, beneficent, firm!
>
> Yes, on some far shining sphere,
> Conscious or not of the past,
> Still thou performest the word
> Of the Spirit in whom thou dost live—
> Prompt, unwearied, as here!

There is one thought of Arnold's in regard to immortality which is distinctive. It is that immortality is a prize to be won. If we fail to win this prize, then, on the principle that nature never wastes anything—an idea then much to the fore—we are ultimately received back into what we may call the cosmic mind-pool from which we were all drawn, as water from a well.[1] Before this takes place we may, in some reincarnation, be given another chance

> To see if we will now at last be true
> To our own only true, deep-buried selves;

[1] Cf. Renan: 'Les méchants et les sots meurent tout entiers.'

but, unless we do overcome in what are successively more difficult lives, we shall be absorbed into the divine, and lose our individuality. To illustrate this best we must quote a lengthy passage from 'Empedocles on Etna'; for, though 'Empedocles' is a dramatic poem, the idea occurs in other of Arnold's poems also, only it is not there so well expressed. This consideration avoids the crude error of quoting a dramatic poem as though it necessarily expressed the mind of the poet.

> To the elements it came from
> Everything will return—
> Our bodies to earth,
> Our blood to water,
> Heat to fire,
> Breath to air.
> They were well born, they will be well entomb'd—
> But mind? . . .

(But for mind Empedocles would be satisfied with pantheistic immortality.)

> And we might gladly share the fruitful stir
> Down in our mother earth's miraculous womb;
> Well would it be
> With what roll'd of us in the stormy main
> We might have joy, blent with the all-bathing air,
> Or with the nimble, radiant life of fire.
> But mind, but thought—
> If these have been the master part of us—
> Where will *they* find their parent element?
> What will receive *them*, who will call *them* home?
> But we shall still be in them, and they in us,
> And we shall be the strangers of the world,
> And they will be our lords, as they are now;
> And keep us prisoners of our consciousness,
> And never let us clasp and feel the All
> But through their forms, and modes, and stifling veils.
> And we shall be unsatisfied as now;
> And we shall feel the agony of thirst,
> The ineffable longing for the life of life

> Baffled for ever; and still thought and mind
> Will hurry us with them on their homeless march,
> Over the unallied unopening earth,
> Over the unrecognizing sea; while air
> Will blow us fiercely back to sea and earth,
> And fire repel us from its living waves.
> And then we shall unwillingly return
> Back to this meadow of calamity,
> This uncongenial place, this human life;
> And in our individual human state
> Go through the sad probation all again,
> To see if we will poise our life at last,
> To see if we will now at last be true
> To our own only true, deep-buried selves,
> Being one with which we are one with the whole world;
> Or whether we will once more fall away
> Into some bondage of the flesh or mind.

This process Empedocles sees going on and on, each succeeding age holding more peril for us than the last; and, unless we overcome, Nature will knead us in her hot hand,

> And we shall feel our powers of effort flag,
> And rally them for one last fight—and fail;
> And we shall sink in the impossible strife,
> And be astray for ever.

Here we have almost the Hindu conception of ceaseless lives until the soul becomes fitted for some kind of fusion with the divine or the All. As a development of the idea we have the thought that repeated incarnations wear out the soul, and that if the soul has to go through a very great number of incarnations its energy may become exhausted and nothing remain for it but annihilation. We get the idea of absorption in 'The River':

> Ah, let me weep, and tell my pain,
> And on thy shoulder rest my head!
> Before I die—before the soul
> Which now is mine, must re-attain
> Immunity from my control,
> And wander round the world again.

That is to say, the soul will drop back into the ocean of being of whose life all life is some kind of manifestation. And in the Epilogue to ' Haworth Churchyard ' there is the similar thought of the vast processes of living nature, which from the ' labour-house vast ' continually throw up new forms of life and take old forms to re-shape them and give them birth in new ways. The poet thinks this may be done in the case of human souls till they are brought back into a new conscious life better than the last.

>   the rain
> Lashes the newly-made grave.
>
> Unquiet souls !
> —In the dark fermentation of earth,
> In the never idle workshop of nature,
> In the eternal movement,
> Ye shall find yourselves again !

The idea of personal immortality as a prize to be won had an attraction for Arnold's austere and robust spirit. To him immortality is not to be thought of as a kind of inevitable panacea, ultimately applied, with unfailing effect, to all the ills of the world. He attacks, we think, the kind of attitude which says, ' What is the use of stirring oneself to right wrong now, whether personal or social ? It will all be put right in another life.' Such an attitude is a drug which puts the soul to sleep. In the Preface to *Last Essays* he writes : ' It is well known how imperfectly and amiss the Jewish nation conceived righteousness. And finally, when their misconceived righteousness failed them in actual life, more and more they took refuge in imaginings about the future, and filled themselves with hopes of a Kingdom of God, a resurrection, a judgement, an eternal life, bringing in and establishing for ever this misconceived righteousness of theirs.' Nor will Arnold accept the thought which is a parallel thought to the one we are considering, namely, that man should give up all hope of making this life fulfil their desires, and rest in the future when their dreams will come true.

> Is it so small a thing
> To have enjoy'd the sun,
> To have lived light in the spring,
> To have loved, to have thought, to have done;
> To have advanced true friends, and beat down baffling foes—
> That we must feign a bliss
> Of doubtful future date,
> And, while we dream on this,
> Lose all our present state,
> And relegate to worlds yet distant our repose?

Both thoughts are dope. Arnold rallies the soul from such somnolence with the challenge that unless it bestirs itself now it may sleep the sleep from which there is no awakening of any kind. The 'powers of effort flag,' he tells us. We may try to rouse ourselves at last, and find it too late:

> And we shall sink in the impossible strife,
> And be astray for ever.

Is not this the meaning of the poem 'Immortality'?

> Foil'd by our fellow-men, depress'd, outworn,
> We leave the brutal world to take its way,
> And, *Patience! in another life*, we say,
> *The world shall be thrust down, and we up-borne.*
>
> And will not, then, the immortal armies scorn
> The world's poor, routed leavings? or will they
> Who fail'd under the heat of this life's day
> Support the fervours of the heavenly morn?
>
> No, no! the energy of life may be
> Kept on after the grave, but not begun;
> And he who flagg'd not in the earthly strife,
> From strength to strength advancing—only he,
> His soul well knit, and all his battles won,
> Mounts, and that hardly, to eternal life.

In a not dissimilar strain, Arnold writes in 'God and

the Bible' to show that 'righteousness' is the only earnest of immortality. Christ's promise of life 'judges not only the life to which men cling here, but just as much the life we love to promise ourselves in the New Jerusalem. The immortality propounded by Jesus must be looked for elsewhere than in the materialistic aspiration of our popular religion.[1] He lived in the eternal order, and the eternal order never dies; this, if we may try to formulate in one sentence the result of the sayings of Jesus about life and death, is the sense in which, according to Him, we can rightly conceive of the righteous man as immortal, *and aspire to be immortal ourselves.*'[2]

Goethe expresses the view that 'he would be immortal who had soul enough to persist.' Plato, in *Phaedo*[3] speculates that the soul may be worn out gradually by successive incarnations, and that possibly a man, without knowing it, may be living his last life before he sinks into nothingness, for the simple reason that his soul may not have risen to that degree of perfection necessary for life with the gods on the one hand, nor has it sufficient energy to undertake another incarnation on earth on the other. So, in 'The Scholar Gipsy,' Arnold says :

> For what wears out the life of mortal men?
> 'Tis that from change to change their being rolls;
> 'Tis that repeated shocks, again, again,
> Exhaust the energy of strongest souls
>   And numb the elastic powers.

[1] In *Literature and Dogma* (p. 366) Arnold pours great scorn on those whose view of heaven is 'a kind of perfected middle-class home, with labour ended, the table spread, goodness all round, the lost ones restored, hymnody incessant.'

[2] Italics ours. Cf. *Literature and Dogma*, p. 367. Arnold says that we have an experience of righteousness which is an experience of life in the truest and deepest sense. 'If this experimental sense does not rise to the sense of being inextinguishable, that is probably because our experience of righteousness is really so very small. . . . We have in our experience this strong sense of life from righteousness to start with; capable of being developed apparently, by progress in righteousness, into something immeasurably stronger. Here is the true basis for all religious aspiration after immortality.'

[3] 87.

Whether it would be just to say that Arnold took the idea from Goethe or Plato, or both, I cannot say. No English poet, however, reflects Goethe as Matthew Arnold does. Nor was any other nineteenth-century poet so familiar with the text of Plato.

Matthew Arnold is a religious seeker who has not been able to harmonize all the inconsistencies of his scheme of thought. He is not orthodox. None of the poets are: a fact which is worth contemplating in the light of Shelley's claims for the poet in the concluding sections of his *Essay on Poetry*. With some ideas which are a part of orthodoxy Arnold will have no dealings at all. The idea of the Trinity, for instance, he dismissed as ' not in the least like what Jesus was in the habit of saying, and just like what would be attributed to Him as baptism and its formula grew in importance.... We ought now rather to keep Trinity Sunday as a day of penitence for the aberrations of theological dogmatists.' He dismisses the three creeds with the amusing titles, ' popular science, learned science, and learned science with a strong dash of temper.' But a man may be very religious without being able intellectually to subscribe to the creeds; just as, conversely, many semi-pagan people in England accept them all

> Vague half-believers in our casual creeds,

as Matthew Arnold calls them.

For Arnold, ' religion is the solidest of realities, and Christianity the greatest and happiest stroke ever yet made for human perfection.' He says that religion makes for man's happiness, but does not rest on that for a motive. It ' finds a far surer ground in personal devotion to Christ ... in believing that Christ is come from God' (query: ' a stream or tendency'), ' following Christ, loving Christ. And in the happiness which this believing in Him, following Him, and loving Him gives, it finds the mightiest of sanctions.' ' Two things about the Christian religion,' he tells us on another occasion, ' must be clear to all persons who have eyes to see ; one is that they cannot do without it, the other that they cannot do with it as it is.' In the Preface to *Last Essays on Church and Religion*, he pleads eloquently, and somewhat wistfully, for some great soul to arise and ' purge the ore of Christianity from the dross.' He himself in past days had essayed this great task. No one knew better than Arnold that in that task he failed. Had he succeeded, then, among other things, we might have had a new eschatology superior to that which we have seen worked out by Tennyson. Perhaps by nature Arnold was the critic rather than the constructive thinker. But he was the seeker. He sought for truth with a moral courage, a fearless honesty, and an intellectual sincerity never excelled in history. His hope was real and never forsook him. But it was a hope born, not of faith, but of reaction from despair. In those wild days of doubt he sailed on, but no port ever appeared in sight. He would not plunge with Empedocles into the crater ; but when he lifted his eyes no friendly star lightened the darkness of his night, or held his spirit steadfast, quiet, and calm. He kept on trusting, with no reason for trusting save the doggedness of the spirit that holds on because it is its nature to hold on. He kept on seeking new worlds for old, and, finding them not, would not return the way he had come. Ultimately, in a religious sense, he failed ; but he never ceased to believe in the possibility of a success he never experienced. Still his work is undone. Still the world waits for some pioneer in the world of thought to

>   fill up the gaps in our files,
>   Strengthen the wavering line,
>   Stablish, continue our march,
>   On, to the bound of the waste,
>   On, to the City of God.

2

Arthur Hugh Clough (1819–1861)

Arthur Hugh Clough is interesting and noteworthy mainly on account of the fact that he is sympathetic with, and symptomatic of, the thinking youth of his day. Far more than Arnold, Clough is the ' Poet of Doubt,'

> Wandering between two worlds, one dead,
> The other powerless to be born.

Passionately religious and highly intellectual, he began, even in early youth, to let the white light of critical inquiry play upon received religion, only to find his faith intellectually untenable in its orthodox form. Yet his religious nature was dissatisfied with every rejection of the intellect. So a conflict in the mind was produced, which was far more severe than any reference to it would seem to suggest. Emotionally he was hungry for the satisfaction of religion. Intellectually he was bound, by his own love of truth and sincerity, to stand aloof. Heart and brain were at war. In 1848, with commendable honesty, he resigned his fellowship at Oriel College, Oxford, and with it his career, because he did not feel at ease in a university which asked its members to subscribe to the Thirty-nine Articles of the Church of England. Having given up so much because of a sceptical outlook on religion, he was not, however, proud of his scepticism. Again and again in his writings he expresses a fear that he may all the time be on the wrong track. The only anchor for his soul seems an utter conviction that truth is, and that it must be followed ardently, whatever the cost may be. Some of his most famous lines are a prayer to God, whose truth is eternal, and who Himself is unchangeable.

> It fortifies my soul to know
> That, though I perish, Truth is so :
> That, howsoe'er I stray and range,
> Whate'er I do, Thou dost not change.
> I steadier step when I recall
> That, if I slip, Thou dost not fall.

We may use Clough's own figure in ' Songs in Absence ' :

> Where lies the land to which the ship would go ?
> Far, far ahead is all her seamen know.
> And where the land she travels from ? Away,
> Far, far behind, is all that they can say—

and think of the lines as making, in some sense, a picture of the voyaging mind of the poet.

If we come, then, to ask what Clough teaches about the idea of immortality, we shall not be surprised to find it vague in the extreme. In this, as in every religious idea he touches, Clough has left the shore of orthodoxy. He has reached no other, though sometimes glimpses of a coast-line break the horizon. He seems to interpret the meaning of his own existence as being

> To gather facts from far and near,
> Upon the mind to hold them clear,
> And, knowing more may yet appear,
> Unto one's latest breath to fear
> The premature result to draw.

So we are not surprised that in a speculative idea like that of immortality we reach no conclusion with Clough.

In 1835 a poem was published in the *Rugby Magazine* called ' The First of the Dead.' It is not included in the published works of the poet. We quote the following lines from it :

And thou art gone, my dear one, the firstling of the grave,
And He hath taken lovingly who bountifully gave.

· · · · · · ·

Joy's sunny day hath passed away, and Sorrow's night hath
  found us ;
But the worlds that glaring lustre hid are beaming now
  around us,
The beauty and the bliss of earth beguilingly they shone,
But the kingdoms of Infinity shine forth in might alone.

But this was written before the period of doubt. It was quickly followed by scepticism. In 1841 he heads some verses ' Blank Misgivings of a Creature Moving about in Worlds not Realized,' beginning :

>Here am I yet, another twelvemonth spent,
>One-third departed of the mortal span,
>Carrying on the child into the man,
>Nothing into reality. Sails rent,
>And rudder broken—reason impotent—
>Affections all unfixed ; so forth I fare
>On the mid seas unheedingly.

The lines to celebrate the twenty-fifth anniversary of the wedding of his friends, Mr. and Mrs. Walrond, of Calder Park, written in 1845, are merely the conventional lines a poet must needs write on such an occasion. They are not to be thought of as indicative of the poet's state of mind :

>Come years again ! as many yet ! and purge
> Less precious earthier elements away,
>And, gently changed at life's extremest verge,
> Bring bright in gold your perfect fiftieth day !
>That sight may children see and parents show !
> If not—yet earthly chains of metal true,
>By love and duty wrought and fixed below,
> Elsewhere will shine, transformed, celestial-new;
>Will shine of gold, whose essence, heavenly bright,
> No doubt-damps tarnish, worldly passions fray ;
>Gold into gold there mirrored, light in light,
> Shall gleam in glories of a deathless day.

Here we have a bald hazarding of some future existence, without any detail, without any basis, without much conviction. Yet, casual and conventional though the lines are, it has to be admitted that they show the high-water mark of the positive idea of immortality in Clough. When that is said, it appears how little we get from Clough on this subject. The positive note has died away in 1851, and it never returns.

> Ah, yet when all is thought and said,
> The heart still overrules the head,
> Still what we hope we must believe,
> And what is given us receive;
>
> Must still believe, for still we hope
> That in a world of larger scope
> What here is faithfully begun
> Will be completed, not undone.
>
> My child, we still must think, when we
> That ampler life together see,
> Some true result will yet appear
> Of what we are, together, here.

Part I. of the poem entitled 'Easter Day' is surely one of the most depressing in English literature, comparable only with Thomson's 'The City of Dreadful Night.'

> Ashes to ashes, dust to dust;
> As of the unjust, also of the just—
> Yea, of that Just One, too!
> This is the one sad Gospel that is true—
> Christ is not risen.

Part II. of the same poem is less negative, and is meant to be an answer to Part I. But the jingle contains little assurance. The poet would seem to hold that, though the physical resurrection of Christ cannot be accepted by the intellect, yet it is possible to accept the idea of Christ's spiritual survival of death.

> Though dead, not dead;
> Not gone, though fled;
> Not lost, though vanished.
> In the great gospel and true creed
> He is yet risen indeed;
> Christ is yet risen.

'Dipsychus' does not help us much. In the first place,

it is a doubtful procedure to affirm that a view expressed by a dramatic character is necessarily the opinion of the poet. And, even if this were permissible, there is little for our quest. The Spirit asks :

> Will you go on thus
> Until death end you ? if indeed it does.
> For what it does, none knows. . . .
> . . . Methinks I see you,
> Through everlasting limbos of void time,
> Twirling and twiddling ineffectively,
> And indeterminately swaying for ever.

The poem entitled ' In the Great Metropolis ' expresses doubt in the same way :

> And after death, we do not know,
> But scarce can doubt, where'er we go,
> The devil takes the hindmost, O !

So also in ' The Stream of Life ' :

> O end to which our currents tend,
> Inevitable sea
> To which we flow, what do we know,
> What shall we guess of thee ?
> A roar we hear upon thy shore,
> As we our course fulfil ;
> Scarce we divine a sun will shine
> And be above us still.

In ' Amours de Voyage,' where we must remember the restriction noted above, the note of doubt is still uppermost (Canto v., Claude to Eustace, vi.) :

Whither depart the souls of the brave that die in the battle,
Die in the lost, lost fight, for the cause that perishes with them ?
Are they upborne from the field on the slumberous pinions
    of angels
Unto a far-off home, where the weary rest from their labour,
And the deep wounds are healed, and the bitter and burning
    moisture
Wiped from the generous eyes ? or do they linger, unhappy,
Pining, and haunting the grave of their by-gone hope and
    endeavour ?

The only poems which Clough wrote with the specific intention of discussing the thoughts of death and a possible after-world are the 'Seven Sonnets on the Thought of Death.' In these he is oppressed with the thought that for the human personality death should be the end:

> for a being that demands the name
> We highest deem—a Person and a Soul—
> It troubles us that this should be the whole;

yet he feels that the instinct which points to immortality may be a pleasant self-deception, which only half deceives the man

> who upon death's immediate brink,
> Knowing, perforce determines to ignore;
> Or than the bird's, that when the hunter's near,
> Burying her eyesight, can forget her fear.

Yet that instinct will not be denied. Immortality has been taught in every age and clime, and man would grasp eagerly at any authority who could assure him of the fact, and would not ask how or where the end was to be accomplished.

So much, then, for Clough's definite references to the idea of immortality. They leave on our mind the impression of a hope, a vague desire; but both are frequently veiled in scepticism, and on occasion Clough becomes a cynic. What one is bound to admire in Clough is his intellectual honesty in seeking the truth in religious problems. A letter written in 1847 illustrates this point. Speaking of the doctrine of the Atonement, he says, ' The evangelicals gabble at it, as the papists do their Ave Marias, and yet say they know; while Newman falls down and worships because he does not know, and knows that he does not know. I think others are more right who say boldly, " We don't understand it, and therefore we won't fall down and worship it." Though there is no reason for adding " there is nothing in it." I should say, " Until I know, I will wait, and, if I am not born with the power to discover, I will do what I can with what knowledge I have—trust to God's justice, and neither pretend to know, nor, without knowing, pretend to embrace, nor yet to oppose those who, by whatever means, are increasing, or trying to increase, knowledge." [1]

Another letter showing Clough's honest and truth-loving mind was written in regard to his resignation as a tutor at Oxford. 'I feel greatly rejoiced to think this is my last term of bondage in Egypt, though I shall, I suppose, quit the fleshpots for a wilderness, with small hope of manna, quails, or water from the rock. . . . One may do worse than hire oneself as a common labourer; 'tis at any rate being honester than being a teacher of Thirty-nine Articles.'[2]

So we find Clough doggedly refusing to accept a comfortable creed, even when his whole soul longed for comfort, since it was, to him, irreconcilable with his intellect. There was one period in his life when this hunger was more than usually poignant. In 1842 Dr. Arnold died. Clough, during his time at Rugby, had been his favourite pupil. The character of the great doctor had made a very deep impression on Clough's mind and heart. When he heard of the doctor's death he left Oxford, went home to Liverpool, and thence to the Welsh hills for a period of solitary wandering. That Dr. Arnold should die at that particular time, when the clamour of the Oxford Movement filled the air, was to Clough a disaster of the first magnitude. The experience, however, produced no 'Rugby Chapel.' It just made our poet more lonely, more wistful, more introspective than ever.

In the same year, 1842, his youngest brother, George, went out to Charleston on his father's business, and died after a few months, aged only twenty-two. The father sailed for America before the news of his son's death reached Liverpool, where the Cloughs

[1] *Poems and Prose Remains*, vol. i., p. 111.
[2] Quoted in *Arthur Hugh Clough*, by Samuel Waddington, p. 127.

were then living. In 1843, Mr. Clough senior returned to England much broken down by grief and ill-health, and died in November 1844. For a great deal of this period the poet was at home, and we are told that, though he did not become morose or alter his main views of life, yet he was known to be pondering very deeply the questions of grief and death. It would be characteristic of him not to shun them, not to minimize or exaggerate them, not to solve them with too easy a philosophy—or the lack of it. At the same time the result of his thinking is negative. There is nothing in creative art born of this experience. His mentality seems to have become like the scenery of his walks round Liverpool during that depressing winter. The Mersey flats, the fog above the river, the November sky, seem to have entered, with their bleakness and dreariness, into his very spirit, producing the vague hope, the infinite longing, the comfortless doubt.

There is one religious view which Clough seems to have held distinctively, and it is positive and definite, to be noted here inasmuch as it is more emphasized than any other religious idea in the poet's writings, and it has a bearing on the subject of immortality. It is that of the immanence of God within the human personality. As Mr. J. A. Symonds has said : ' Clough simply tried to reduce belief to its original and spiritual purity, to lead men back to the God that is within them, witnessed by their consciences and by the history of the human race.' That view of God seemed to Clough sufficient.

> O Thou in that mysterious shrine
> Enthroned, as I must say, divine !
> I will not frame one thought of what
> Thou mayest either be or not.
> I will not prate of ' thus ' or ' so,'
> And be profane with ' yes ' or ' no ' ;
> Enough that in our soul and heart
> Thou, whatsoe'er Thou may'st be, art.

Only as confirmatory of ideas already expressed in other poems is it permissible, we think, to quote a dramatic poem. But, with this proviso, some words of Adam in ' Fragments of the Mystery of the Fall ' are interesting.

Eve :
    O Adam, I can scarcely think I hear ;
    For if God said to us—God being God—
    ' You shall not,' is not His Commandment His ?
    And are we not the creatures He hath made ?

Adam .
    My child, God does not speak to human minds
    In that unmeaning arbitrary way ;
    God were not God if so, and good not good.
    Search in your heart, and if you tell me there
    You find a genuine voice—no fancy, mind you—
    Declaring to you this or that is evil,
    Why, this or that I daresay evil is.
    Believe me, I will listen to the word ;
    For not by observation of without
    Cometh the kingdom of the voice of God :
    It is within us—let us seek it there.
      .   .   .   .   .
    God's voice is of the heart : I do not say
    All voices, therefore, of the heart are God's ;
    And to discern the voice amid the voices
    Is that hard task, my love, that we are born to.

If God, then, dwells within the human spirit in so intimate a way that the latter is an expression of the divine—an expression hindered, hampered, and limited by the human personality, by its stage of development, and by its material medium, yet a real expression, man being different, not in kind, but only in degree, from God—then we have a strong case for immortality. Man must be, on this hypothesis, partly spirit, and over spirit physical death can be conceived as having no power.

Clough, however, does not work out this implication of his own views, and we have no right to do so for him and charge him with the result. His contribution to our thought on immortality must always remain that of doubt. One imagines that, if one had pressed him concerning the implications of the idea expressed above, he would have turned to one and drearily quoted his own lines in ' The Questioning Spirit ' :

> Truly, thou know'st not, and thou need'st not know ;
> Hope only, hope thou, and believe alway ;
> I also know not, and I need not know ;
> Only with questionings pass I to and fro,
> Perplexing these that sleep, and in their folly
> Imbreeding doubt and sceptic melancholy.

3

Algernon Charles Swinburne (1837–1909)

The study of Swinburne in the attempt to discover his conception of immortality is perhaps the most exhilarating of all those we have made in regard to the poets of the century. The reason for this is that in one poem we find Tennyson called

> the black negation of the bier,

and in the next we find an assurance that death cannot be the end. Examples of this fact, and an attempted explanation of it, we shall leave for the moment ; but it seems important to state it at the outset.

The problem of immortality has its religious, as well as its philosophical, aspect. The poet's general attitude to religion, therefore, will not be an irrelevant consideration. It will be one of the influences likely to modify his conception.

It may be stated with little fear of contradiction that Swinburne had no interest in theology, the science of religion. T. H. Green describes a meeting of the Old Mortality Club at Oxford, where he read a paper on the development of Christian dogma. While reading, he happened to look up from his paper, and was almost overcome with laughter at the sight of Swinburne, whose face 'wore an expression compounded of unutterable ennui and naïve astonishment that men whom he respected could take an interest in such a subject.'[1]

Unlike Clough, Swinburne did not find in the practical observance of religion any satisfaction for his soul. At Oxford he was continually 'gated,' we are told, for defiantly neglecting morning chapel. And at the end of his life he left instructions—which were disregarded—that the Prayer Book service for the Burial of the Dead was not to be read at his funeral, since he did not believe in what it implied and stated. Antagonism seems to have been the only evidence of his interest in religion, and of that antagonism he was inordinately proud. On one occasion he wrote, 'I have written a modern companion-in-arms and metre to my "Hymn to Proserpine," called "Hymn of Man," by the side of which "Queen Mab" is, as it were, an archdeacon's charge, and my own previous blasphemies are models of Christian devotion.' This antagonism, one feels, is partly a pose. Swinburne himself said that he had ' a touch of Byronic ambition to be thought an eminent and terrible enemy to the decorous life and respectable fashion of the world'; and, as in Byron's case, ' a sincere scorn and horror of hypocrisy' was mingled with a boyish and voluble affection of 'audacity and excess.' One suspects the influence of this love of shocking the susceptibilities of the pious in such lines as :

All we are against Thee, against Thee, O God most High,

in ' Atlanta in Calydon ' ; and

What ailed us, O gods, to desert you
For creeds that refuse and restrain ?

[1] *Algernon Charles Swinburne*, Edmund Gosse, p. 40.

in ' Dolores ' ; and the following lines in the beautiful ' Hymn to Proserpine ' :

Wilt thou take all, Galilean ? but these Thou shalt not take,
The laurel, the palms, and the paean, the breasts of the nymphs in the brake ;
Breasts more soft than a dove's . . .

. . . .

Thou hast conquered, O pale Galilean ; the world has grown grey from thy breath.

Probably it flattered this affected pose of the poet that the devout Christina Rossetti, in her copy of ' Atalanta,' pasted a piece of paper over the words ' the supreme evil, God.' Manifestations of the same pose are seen in the disparaging references made to Tennyson's ' Idylls of the King ' and ' Morte D'Arthur,' and ' the lewd circle of strumpets and adulterers revolving round the central figure of their inane wittol.' And on one occasion, at a supper-party, Swinburne declared that if he could indulge his whim he would build a castle with seven towers, and in each of the towers daily should be enacted one of the seven deadly sins !

Yet his antagonism was not all pose. At the same time it may be said in all fairness that it was directed against the formality and conventionality of religion rather than against its spirit. Swinburne hated anything which even remotely savoured of priestcraft, or sought by external authority to impose belief of any kind on men's minds, and thus coerce a kind of intellectual assent which, to Swinburne, just because it was coerced, was the worst form of tyranny on the one hand and the worst form of insincerity on the other. Edward Thomas, in his book on the poet, says : ' As to the formal religious currents in his time, he could seldom speak of them with civility, and there is no reason for doubting that he shared the feeling of the singer of the " Hymn to Proserpine " about

ghastly glories of saints, dead limbs of gibbeted Gods.

It is probable that his nature and his extraordinary gift of rich metaphor led him to express himself in a way which his maturer judgement would fain have softened down.' He himself in later years referred to his earlier poems as 'sins of youth'; but there is no evidence for saying that he ever became in any sense a religious man.

As to Christianity, he had no quarrel with Christ, but he would never have admitted His divinity. Gosse tells us that ' the only degree to which Swinburne to the very end of his life approached Christianity was in his reiterated expressions of reverence for Christ as the type of human aspiration and perfection. " Jesus may have been the highest and purest sample of man on record," he would grant, and this was the limit of his acquiescence.'[1] This testimony is borne out by the poet's reply to critics of his two sonnets on the death of Louis Napoleon, bearing the title ' The Descent into Hell.' He says that he could only have offended 'those to whom the name of Christ and all memories connected with it are hateful, and those to whom the name of Bonaparte and all memories connected with it are not. I belong to neither class.'

Some words of Clara Watts-Dunton, wife of Swinburne's self-appointed guardian, are relevant here, for they carry us from the point we have now reached to a discussion of what the poet thought of the life after death. In her book, *The Home Life of Swinburne*,[2] she says: 'I do not believe that Swinburne in his heart of hearts was so violently agnostic and opposed to Christianity as the hatred of the crimes of bigotry has led people to think. His letters to his mother, in the book by his cousin, Mrs. Leith, *The Boyhood of A. C. Swinburne*, show what sane and sweet ideas regarding the after-life he entertained. To her

---

[1] Gosse, op. cit., 310. Swinburne's line in ' A New Year Ode ':
    ' The grave that heard the clarion call of Christ,'
though interesting, is so solitary that it is unsafe to deduce anything from it.
[2] p. 269.

whom he loved so dearly he wrote in 1892, " It is so beautiful and delightful to think of ' being together when this life is over,' as you say, and seeing things no longer ' in a glass darkly,' and all who have ever tried to do a little bit of what they thought right being brought together—if what they thought right was not absolutely wicked and shocking, like the beliefs of persecutors, and understanding and loving each other—that I sometimes feel as if it ought hardly to be talked about." Undoubtedly,' Mrs. Watts-Dunton adds, ' Swinburne did not deny the existence of a life beyond the grave.'

The poet also wrote to his mother in 1885, just after the death of Victor Hugo, as follows : ' When I think of his intense earnestness of faith in a future life and a better world than this, and remember how fervently Mazzini always urged upon all who loved him the necessity of that belief and the certainty of its actual truth, I feel very deeply that they must have been right—or at least that they should have been—however deep and difficult the mystery which was so clear and transparent to their inspired and exalted minds may seem to such as mine.'

Yet, when we apply the acid test and ask what was the poet's reaction to the experience of the death of one whom he loved deeply, we find that in 1877, when his father died, he simply said that he ' knew not ' if the dead one's life and spirit and work ' here are done.'

Turning to the poems, we find that there is one thing that is very noteworthy in the poet's attitude to death. It is never feared. It is never dreaded. It is never looked upon as an enemy. It is always referred to with courage and cheerfulness. It may be regarded as the end, but, if so, it is a welcome end, bringing peace and release, if only in nothingness.

> For thee, O now a silent soul, my brother,
> Take at my hands this garland, and farewell.
> Thin is the leaf, and chill the wintry smell,
> And chill the solemn earth, a fatal mother,

158   THE AFTER-WORLD OF THE POETS

> With sadder than the Niobean womb,
> And in the hollow of her breasts a tomb.
> Content thee, howsoe'er, whose days are done,
> There lies not any troublous thing before,
> Nor sight nor sound to war against thee more,
> For whom all winds are quiet as the sun,
> All waters as the shore.[1]

Death may often be thought of as the beginning, and, if so, it is the beginning of a fairer life.

> the dawn of death, whose light makes dim
> The starry fires that life sees rise and set.
> .   .   .   .
>   how high the freed soul climbs
> That death sets free from change of day and night.
> .   .   .   .
> The dead whom death and twin-born fame deliver
> From life that dies, and time's inveterate sway.
> .   .   .   .
> And eastward now, and ever towards the dawn,
> If death's deep veil by life's bright hand be rent,
> We see, as though the shadow of death withdrawn,
> The imperious soul's indomitable ascent.[2]

And, again, in 'Via Dolorosa' (Deliverance):

> O Death, fair Death, sole comforter and sweet,
> Nor Love nor Hope can give such gifts as thine.
>   . . . Night has given what day
> Denied him : darkness hath unsealed his eyes;

and in 'The Order of Release':

>   Grace enough is ours
> To know that pain for him has fallen on rest.
> The worst we know was his on earth : the best,
> We fain would think,—a thought no fear deflowers—
> Is his, released from bonds of rayless hours.

In this happy view it may be that Swinburne mirrors

[1] 'Ave atque Vale,' xviii.   [2] 'Elegy.'

Landor, for whom we know he had a veneration amounting to hero-worship. Landor, at the age of ninety, had a conversation with Swinburne touching the approach of death. The former said that he had no belief in the immortality of the soul, nor opinion about it; but of one thing he was certain, ' that whatsoever was to come was best—the right thing, or the thing that ought to come.' It is the present writer's opinion that Swinburne, perhaps unconsciously, adopted the same attitude, which we may call a kind of optimistic agnosticism.

No one could claim that his closing words in the *Essay on Byron* (1866) speak of what is commonly called the ' Christian hope '; yet there is an undefinable note of optimism and cheerfulness in those famous and faultless sentences. ' Few can ever have gone wearier to the grave; none with less fear. He had done enough to earn his rest. Forgetful now, and set free for ever from all faults and foes, he passed through the doorway of no ignoble death out of reach of time, out of sight of love, out of hearing of hatred, beyond the blame of England and the praise of Greece. In the full strength of spirit and of body his destiny overtook him and made an end of all his labours. He had seen, and borne, and achieved, more than most men on record. " He was a great man, good at many things, and now he had attained this also, to be at rest." '

This optimistic agnosticism is well illustrated from the ' Lake of Gaube ' :

> But well shall it be with us ever
> Who drive through the darkness here,
> If the soul that we live by never,
> For aught that a lie saith, fear;[1]

and from the lines concerning the blind poet, Marston, where human nature desires to realize again the

---

[1] The ' lie' referred to being, one supposes, the false teaching of the ' priest ' concerning eternal punishment.

presence on earth of the dead friend, but at the same time realizes that he is far better where he is, and

> Would not love him so worse than ill,
> Would not clothe him again with care.'[1]

The same idea occurs in 'Via Dolorosa' (Transfiguration) :

> What hearts were ours who loved him, should we pray
>   That night would yield him back to darkling day,
> Sweet death that soothes, to life that spoils and smites ?
> For now, perchance, life, lovelier than the light's
>   That shed no comfort on his weary way
> Shows him what none may dream to see or say
>   Ere yet the soul may scale those topless heights
>   Where death lies dead.

We come now to the most important aspect of Swinburne's eschatology. How are we to account for the diversity of statements? In one poem, as we hinted in the first paragraph, he will blankly deny any further life at all for the human spirit. In another he will frankly affirm it, and even go further. He will describe aspects of it. Again, in one poem the language will be that of a Christian mystic, in another that of a pantheist, in another that of a pagan polytheist, in another that of an atheist.

Every poet is profoundly influenced by the mood he is in when he is writing the poem. The poet may be so carried beyond himself that his own personal opinions are lost sight of, varied, and even contradicted. But, for most poets, their private convictions influence their most ecstatic moods, and may be detected beneath them. A good example of this is seen in the case of Tennyson and Browning, who could never, even in a dramatic poem, have left the final impression on the mind of the reader that death was the end of all. Their personal conviction in regard to immortality was too strong.

[1] 'Threnody.'

Of Browning, Professor Henry Jones said: ' He is, as a rule, conscious of no theory; . . . nevertheless, it may be shown that a theory rules him from behind, and that profound convictions arise in the heart and rush along the blood at the moment of creation, using his soul as an instrument of expression to his age and people.'[1]

We believe that, in the case of Swinburne, his convictions were so amorphous that they readily and completely took the shape of his mood when writing. We find this even in his prose. He writes to his mother and we find him looking forward to a life beyond death. On another occasion we find him writing that the immortality of the soul is an ' utterly incognizable matter on which it is equally unreasonable to have, or to wish to have, an opinion.'

In his poetry we find the same thing in a more marked degree. The conviction is so nebulous that the mood of the moment has entire authority over it. When he writes after the death of his friends, he will not let death have the last word. He will begin, perhaps, with the only conviction he can ever be said to have held about death:

> Peace, rest, and sleep are all we know of death.

But before long the mood of the poem is giving a far different shape to his own conception.

> Peace, rest, and sleep are all we know of death,
> And all we dream of comfort: yet for thee,
> Whose breath of life was bright and strenuous breath,
> We think the change is other than we see.
>
> The seal of sleep set on thine eyes to-day
> Surely can seal not up the keen swift light
> That lit them once for ever. Night can sláy
> None save the children of the womb of night.

[1] Sir Henry Jones, *Browning as a Philosophical and Religious Teacher*, p. 26.

> The fire that burns up dawn to bring forth noon
> Was father of thy spirit: how should'st thou
> Die as they die for whom the sun and moon
> Are silent? Thee the darkness holds not now.
>
> . . . .
>
> Thou hast swum too soon the sea of death: for us
> Too soon, but if truth bless love's blind belief
> Faith, born of hope and memory, says not thus:
> And joy for thee for me should mean not grief.
>
> And joy for thee, if ever soul of man
> Found joy in change and life of ampler birth
> Than here pens in the spirit for a span,
> Must be the life that doubt calls death on earth.
>
> For if, beyond the shadow and the sleep,
> A place there be for souls without a stain,
> Where peace is perfect and delight more deep
> Than seas or skies that change and shine again,
>
> Then none of all unsullied souls that live
> May hold a surer station: none may lend
> More light to hope's or memory's lamp, nor give
> More joy than thine to those that called thee friend.[1]

The 'Memorial Verses' on the death of Théophile Gautier strike a note hardly less confident:

> through the white gates where rule the deathless dead
> The sound of a new singer's soul was shed
> That sang among his kinsfolk, and a beam
> Shot from the star on a new ruler's head.
>
> A new star lighting the Lethean stream,
> A new song mixed into the song supreme.

So Hugo is spoken of as joining 'the company of his equals'; Landor rejoins 'his kin among the Grecian shades where Orpheus and where Homer are.' 'If,' says Swinburne, 'as some thinkers and dreamers might venture to hope, those two great poets of the

---

[1] 'In Memory of John William Inchbold.'

grave, John Webster and Victor Hugo, have now met in a world beyond the grave . . .' He imagines Tennyson and Shakespeare united. Trelawney rejoins Shelley.

> Heart of hearts, art thou moved not, hearing
> Surely, if hearts of the dead may hear,
> Whose true heart it is now draws near?
> Surely the sense of it thrills thee, cheering
> Darkness and death with the news now nearing—
> Shelley, Trelawney rejoins thee here.[1]

P. B. Marston ' haply ' rejoins Milton, and of Aurelio Saffi he writes:

> He too now hears the heaven we hear not sing.

> He too now dwells where death is dead, and stands
> Where souls like stars exult in life to be;

in

> The deathless life of death which earth calls heaven.[2]

Of Mazzini he writes:

> Above the fume and foam of time that flits,
> The soul, we know
> Now sits on high where Alighieri sits
> With Angelo.

> Not his own heavenly tongue hath heavenly speech
> Enough to say
> What this man was, whose praise no thought may reach,
> No words can weigh.[3]

There is the
> life that is mightier than death[4]

for William Morris and Burne-Jones; and the death of Sir Richard Burton suggests to him that death is a

[1] ' Lines on the Death of Edward John Trelawney.'
[2] ' In Memory of Aurelio Saffi.'
[3] ' Lines on the Monument of Guiseppe Mazzini.'
[4] Dedication to ' A Channel Passage.'

deliverance ' from life that dies.' Of Browning he says that he

> awakened out of life wherein we sleep.

Theodore de Banville ' dies and casts off death ' ; Marston is ' healed of life.' When Mrs. Lynn Linton dies, he asks :

> Has Landor seen that brave, bright smile
> Alive again ?

and he speculates concerning the reunion of father and daughter in the same poem :

> The sire and daughter, twain and one
> In quest and goal,
> Stand face to face beyond the sun,
> And soul to soul.

We see, then, that almost every memorial poem breathes the spirit of, if it does not express belief in, the survival by the human soul of bodily death. There are possible exceptions, as where he speaks of James Norman Graham going at death

> to the dark where all is done ;

but these remain exceptions. Occasionally a beautiful picture of another world is painted, and he shows us

> the garden of death, where the singers whose names are deathless

One with another make music unheard of men,

and

> the beautiful, veiled bright world where the glad ghosts meet.

But it would not be sound to draw a conclusion from these instances as to the convictions of the poet. *All the above quotations are taken from memorial verses.* The mood of Swinburne determines his convictions. That, at least, is our contention. He is almost bound by convention to write memorial verses with some kind of admission of a further life. Moreover, the expressions about various poets rejoining their kin in a further life may often be a figure of speech, meaning that they all now belong to the category of the dead. We note, moreover, in Swinburne, the repetition of the terms of doubt—' *if* death do its trust no wrong'; '*if* the dead be alive'; '*if* ever a voice may be the same in heaven'; '*if* life there be that flies not'; '*if* aught beyond sweet sleep be hidden.' He is never quite sure

> If death be or life be a lie.

We feel that the mood dictates the conviction also in those poems in which Swinburne glorified childhood. He was extremely fond of children, and he cannot write of them as though death meant annihilation.

> A little soul scarce fledged for earth
> Takes wing with heaven again for goal
> Even while we hailed as fresh from birth
> A little soul.
>
> . . . . . .
>
> The little feet that never trod
> Earth, never strayed in field or street,
> What hand leads upwards back to God
> The little feet?
>
> . . . .
>
> What gift has death, God's servant, brought
> The little hands?[1]

We feel the same mood in ' A Baby's Epitaph ':

Angels, calling from your brawling world one undefiled,
Homeward bade me, and forbade me here to rest beguiled:
Here I sleep not: pass, and weep not here upon your child.

The poem 'To a Baby Kinswoman' shows the poet picturing the child's mother still watching over her:

> Child, whose mother's love-lit eyes
> Watch thee from Paradise.
>
> . . . . . .
>
> Love, bowed down for thee to bless,
> Dares not call thee motherless.

[1] 'A Baby's Death.'

Such a conception of life after death as we have seen Swinburne's to be is artistic rather than philosophical. The very existence of his after-world, as well as its quality, depends on his mood. If he is writing dramatically, the after-world suits the character. Chastelard reflects that he is to go ' where a man lies with all his loves put out, and his lips full of earth '; and one feels there is a kind of appropriateness about this. Iseult is willing to go to hell if her lover can be with God, or, if he is to go to hell also, then she will comfort him there. The lover in ' The Triumph of Time ' wants to be buried with his false mistress,

> Clasped and clothed in the cloven clay
> Out of the world's way, out of the light.

The poet himself, than whom perhaps there has never been a more passionate lover of the sea, speaks of returning in death to his ' mother,' and moving with the tide which moves the ships:

> But when my time shall be,
> O mother, O my sea,
> Alive or dead, take me,
> Me too, my mother.

The most famous poem of Swinburne's which deals with our subject is ' Ave atque Vale ' (1867), which he wrote on reading in a French newspaper a report, which turned out to be false, of the death of Charles Baudelaire. On finding that the report was false, Swinburne was about to tear up the MS., but fortunately thrust it into a drawer and produced it when Baudelaire died eleven years later. Gosse calls this poem ' the most highly finished of all his elegiacal poems. . . . This grave and stately threnody has a soberness, a dignity, which distinguish it among the fervid writings of its author. Nowhere else has Swinburne come nearer to the majesty and depth of emotion of the purest Greek literature, nor clothed his thought in severer language'; and Gosse would make it the fourth great elegiac poem in the English language, with 'Lycidas,' 'Adonais,' and 'Thyrsis.'

Beautiful as the poem is from a euphonic point of view, its beauty is only to be gathered, we think, by reading it aloud. So beautiful is its language that one finds oneself ceasing to ask what it means, the critical faculties being in abeyance, the aesthetic in the ascendant. Death is beautiful, and the gateway to a hazy something. In a sentence the whole poem illustrates our former point of the optimistic agnosticism in Swinburne's thought regarding the after-life.

> Now the dim gods of death have in their keeping
> Spirit and body and all the springs of song.
>   . . . .
> Is it not well where soul from body slips?

The uncertainty does not preclude the possibility of cessation of existence:

> For thee no fruits to pluck, no palms for winning,
> No triumph and no labour and no lust,
> Only dead yew-leaves and a little dust.

But the dead is pursued by wondering questions:

> Hast thou found place at the great knees and feet
> Of some pale Titan-woman like a lover,
> Such as thy vision here solicited,
> Under the shadow of her fair vast head,
> The deep division of prodigious breasts,
> The solemn slope of mighty limbs asleep,
> The weight of awful tresses that still keep
> The savour and the shade of old-world pine-forests
> Where the wet hill-winds weep?
>   . . . .
> What of life is there, what of ill or good?
> Are the fruits grey like dust or bright like blood?
> Does the dim ground grow any seed of ours,
> The faint fields quicken any terrene root?

168 THE AFTER-WORLD OF THE POETS

And then, in a mood almost pantheistic, the quest is given up in the most beautiful stanza in the poem :

> Thou art far too far for wings of words to follow,
> Far too far off for thought or any prayer.
> What ails us with thee, who art wind and air ?
> What ails us gazing where all seen is hollow ?
> Yet with some fancy, yet with some desire,
> Dreams pursue death as winds a flying fire,
> Our dreams pursue our dead and do not find.
> Still, and more swift than they, the thin flame flies,
> The low light fails us in elusive skies,
> Still the foiled earnest ear is deaf, and blind
>   Are still the eluded eyes.

It is a beautiful poem, but it does not develop any definite idea of the immortality of the soul.

In yet another mood, Swinburne entirely denies immortality.

> I am tired of tears and laughter,
>   And men that laugh and weep ;
> Of what may come hereafter
>   For men that sow to reap.
>   . . . . .
> Though one were strong as seven,
>   He too with death shall dwell,
> Nor wake with wings in heaven,
>   Nor weep for pains in hell.
>   . . . . .
> We are not sure of sorrow,
>   And joy was never sure ;
> To-day will die to-morrow ;
>   Time stoops to no man's lure ;
> And love, grown faint and fretful,
> With lips but half regretful,
> Sighs, and with eyes forgetful,
>   Weeps that no loves endure.
>
> From too much love of living,
>   From hope and fear set free,
> We thank with brief thanksgiving
>   Whatever gods may be

> That no life lives for ever;
> That dead men rise up never,
> That even the weariest river
>   Winds somewhere safe to sea.
>
> Then star nor sun shall waken,
>   Nor any change of light;
> Nor sound of waters shaken,
>   Nor any sound or sight;
> Nor wintry leaves nor vernal,
> Nor days nor things diurnal,
> Only the sleep eternal
>   In an eternal night.[1]

Death is the end also in ' The Pilgrimage of Pleasure ' :

> Alas! the light in your eyes, the gold in your golden hair!
> Alas! your sayings wise, and the goodly things ye were!
> Alas! your glory, alas! the sound of your names among men!
> Behold, it is come to pass, ye shall sleep and arise not again;
> Dust shall fall on your face, and dust shall hang in your hair;
> Ye shall sleep without shifting of place, and shall be no more as ye were;
> Ye shall never open your mouth; ye shall never lift up your head;
> Ye shall look not to north or to south; life is done; and behold, you are dead.

So we are faced with the problem as to which is the real Swinburne. Is it the poet who in memorial verses, though he never describes another life, yet again and again assumes its existence? Is it the poet who cannot let a little child slip, at death, into nothingness? Is it the poet who gives thanks

>   That no life lives for ever?

The answer is that all are Swinburne. For ourselves, we believe—and it can only be a matter of personal opinion—that we are nearer the essential and characteristic Swinburne in ' The Garden of Proserpine ' than

---

[1] ' The Garden of Proserpine.'

in any other poem. First, because this is better poetry than any of the memorial verses. Second, because there is no conventional restraint to be considered. Third, because the poem seems to us to mirror the spirit of the poet as one gathers it from reading the whole of his poems and several biographies.

The only conclusion we can come to in summing up is that Swinburne gives us no reason for supposing that he ever reached what can be called a definite personal conviction. He writes as his moods dictate. But we think his mind tended in the direction of denial rather than in that of affirmation.

M. Paul de Reul, in one of the best books on the poet, *L'Œuvre de Swinburne*, well sums up the attitude of the poet to immortality : ' Les songeries de Swinburne devant la mort expriment tantôt des aspirations, tantôt des doutes et des ignorances. Cependant si l'on groupe ces poèmes, on y reconnaîtra moins des idées contradictoires que les moments divers d'une pensée qui se cherche et ne se manifeste pas chaque fois en entier ; qui, tout en oscillant dans certaines limites, revient se fixer vers une région préférée.'[1] And to the question whether Swinburne did, or did not, believe in the immortality of the soul, he writes : ' Nous répondrons qu'il croyait à l'esprit, c'est à dire à ce qui ne meurt point, mais n'eut jamais une foi bien solide en l'immortalité individuelle malgré l'exemple de ses maîtres, Mazzini et Hugo.'[2]

[1] p. 255.   [2] p. 253.

V

THE CLIMAX OF DEVELOPMENT

(BROWNING, 1812–1889)

V

THE CLIMAX OF DEVELOPMENT

BROWNING, 1812–1889

I

THE main interest in life for Robert Browning was the human soul—its joys and sorrows, its hopes and fears, its failure and its success. He was the high priest of the humanity of his century. He voiced its needs and aspirations. He faced, with a magnificent faith, its problems. He understood human nature as no other poet has understood it since Shakespeare. It is this perception which, to a large extent, constitutes the appeal of his poetry.

In order to emphasize one aspect of his work we must not disparage another. Like every true poet, Browning extolled beauty wherever he found it. Examples of his love of nature rush to the mind in protest against any attempt to emphasize another aspect by denying this. Spite of all his metaphysical speculations, he knew when it was June,

> when harebells grow,
> And all that kings could ever give or take
> Would not be precious as those blooms to me.[1]

At the same time, his attitude is seen in his own answer to a friend who asked him, ' Do you care for nature much ? ' ' Yes ' said Browning, ' a great deal ; but for human beings a great deal more.' Browning

[1] ' Paracelsus.'

would, I think, have given his consent to the words of Victor Hugo in *Les Misérables*[1] : ' The mind's eye can nowhere find anything more dazzling nor more dark than in man ; it can fix itself upon nothing which is more awful, more complex, more mysterious, or more infinite. There is one spectacle grander than the sea—that is the sky ; there is one spectacle grander than the sky—that is the interior of the soul.'

Nor was Browning's interest so much in human nature in the mass. His persistent use of the dramatic monologue shows his interest in the individual soul. And if that soul manifests eccentricities, peculiarities, possibilities of climbing to the heights or descending to the depths of human experience, so much the better. The ordinary homely lives of ordinary men and women, bound by ordinary bonds of kinship, do not attract him as they attract other poets. Browning could no more have written ' Enoch Arden ' than Tennyson could have written ' The Ring and the Book.'

One of the reasons for this preference was that the human soul gave Browning the kind of problem upon which his brilliant metaphysical mind loved to brood and speculate. Especially in the manifestations of its unusual forms of activity it gave him a field for the kind of study to which he was temperamentally inclined. To him human psychology was a great continent waiting, asking, to be explored, and untiringly, with ever unquenched enthusiasm, he threw his whole mental energy into that quest.

He leads us at one moment up to the mountain heights of the mind of a Paracelsus. He leads us down, at another moment into the murky morasses of the mentality of a Guido. He leads us through the smiling, happy meadows which echo with the glad laughter of a Pippa, and then through a dim, mysterious valley, among half-lights and weird shadows, along whose

[1] Vol. i., p. 80.

tortuous windings flits the ghost of Mr. Sludge. And, whatever may be said of those who follow him, the guide is always quite at home and master of the situation. He writes to Milsand of Dijon, to whom ' Sordello' is dedicated : 'The historical decoration was purposely of no more importance than a background requires ; and my stress lay on the incidents in the development of a soul : *little else is worth study.* I at least always thought so.'

2

Nor is it enough to say that Browning is merely a student of souls. He is a lover of human souls. He is one of those rare spirits who look for the best in the worst ; not by shutting the eyes to the worst, but by realizing that the worst is not all ; indeed, that the worst is often evidence of the possibility of the better. Browning never falls into the facile error of affixing an obvious label to a personality, and then supposing that the label accounts for the entire contents. He will take infinite care to search out the good and expose it, acknowledge it and glorify it. Mr. Sludge is a good example of this. Browning's face would go white with passion whenever Home's name was mentioned— Home being the name of a rather doubtful kind of spiritualist who greatly worked on the credulity and temperamental susceptibilities of Mrs. Browning. Yet, if the contention be true that Mr. Sludge is based on Home, we find Browning patiently dissecting that strange character and giving Sludge the credit for believing that his spiritualism was not *all* fraud, and for being at heart a man. So generously, indeed, does Browning carry out this work that the second part of the monologue has been construed by some readers into a genuine plea for the theory and practice of spiritualism, though nothing could be further from Browning's intention.

Browning is always doing this glorious kind of dissection. In three sentences we may sum up his attitude. He sees the worst in men, and is sympathetic. He sees the best, and believes in it. He teaches that only by believing in the best, in face of the worst, can man's possibilities be made actualities.[1]

Humanity, with its joys and sorrows, hopes and fears, beliefs and doubts, provided the material for Browning's artistic work. When he was composing 'Paracelsus' in 1834, his delight was to walk at night in a wood near Dulwich, whence he could catch the glow, in the sky, of London lights. The thought of the multitude who lived in that glare inspired him.

All this is not irrelevant, we think, in approaching Browning's conception of immortality. The poet who is passionately interested in human souls, who finds the most unpromising worthy of study and meriting love, is likely to give us a view of that soul's immortality in which these considerations play their part. Without unduly anticipating, and without deducing anything from them, we are not surprised to find such lines as those written after the poet has stood in the Paris Morgue before the corpses of three men who had thrown themselves into the Seine one night in the summer of 1856. His great heart is full of pity for them—

> Poor men, God made, and all for that!—

and his conclusion takes him out into another world to explain the puzzle:

> My own hope is, a sun will pierce
> The thickest cloud earth ever stretched;
> That, after Last, returns the First,
> Though a wide compass round be fetched;
> That what began best, can't end worst,
> Nor what God blessed once, prove accurst.[2]

---

[1] 'He was a kind of cosmic detective who walked into the foulest of thieves' kitchens and accused men publicly of virtue.'—G. K. Chesterton, *Robert Browning*, p. 52.
[2] 'Apparent Failure.'

3

Another preliminary consideration which we may briefly survey concerns the poet's attitude to a question the nature of which is religious. Can we say at once that his approach is that of the orthodox Christian apologist? A good many Browningites would unhesitatingly and dogmatically assert that Browning was the Christian poet *par excellence*. He himself would have us hesitate. It may be well to recall that Mr. A. C. Cook, in his *Commentary on the 'Ring and the Book'* (p. 220), writes that Mr. Robert Buchanan reports that, when asked 'categorically' whether he was or was not a Christian, Browning immediately thundered, 'No!' 'But,' adds Mr. Cook, 'the poet was often unfortunate in his reporters, who would understand ἁπλῶς what was meant to be understood as subject to important qualification. The evidence of his poetry shows that his " No " should have been so understood; his " thunder " may have been due to a cause of which the indiscreet questioner was serenely unconscious.'

Let us investigate the question. We think that, *concerning the poet's early work*, two things can be said with little fear of contradiction. His interest in, and love for, the human soul were not motived by ' Christian brotherly love.' It was inevitable, Browning being the kind of man he was. Secondly, his teaching about the human soul here and hereafter had its source in poetic vision, only very slightly coloured by specifically Christian influence.

Then something happened. Professor Herford tells us that ' no single poem written before 1850 shows that acute interest in the problems of the Christian faith which constantly emerges in the work of this and the following years.'[1] Not that the earlier work is hostile to Christianity, but rather that Browning is not

---

[1] Professor C. H. Herford, *Robert Browning*, p. 113.

interested in specifically religious questions. 'Saul,' which at first thought might seem to be an exception to this view, illustrates it. For, though the first nine sections were written in 1845, the later sections, in which the inspired shepherd boy prophesies the manifestation of God in Christ, were written after 1850. This significant new note in Browning's poetry is unquestionably largely due to his wife's influence. She was not a dogmatic or conventional Christian. In her own phrase, she, like her husband, would not wear 'any of the liveries of the sects.'[1]

Yet, though she thought of truth as beyond the power of any creed to capture and embody, she had an intense personal piety, and this had tremendous influence over her husband, as the letters between them show.

Probably Miss Barrett roused the sleeping fires first kindled by the early training of what was perhaps an ideal Christian home. It is worth remembering that Browning's father and mother were both deeply religious people, and Browning says of himself that in his youth he was 'passionately religious.' Yet in that early home was no mere narrow-minded bigotry such as drove Shelley to his miscalled atheism. Robert was allowed—howbeit with some laments from his father— to steep himself in his hero Byron, and one day when he lighted on 'Mr. Shelley's Atheistical Poem' ('Queen Mab'), advertised thus on a bookstall, he was allowed to buy and read it, and his mother afterwards procured for him all the other works of Shelley then obtainable.

We need not over-estimate either influence, but, by February 1846, Browning is found agreeing with his wife's convictions, including one which was regarded as central by both, and 'the most beautiful in the Christian doctrine'—namely, the revelation of God in Christ. So the poet begins to write in a more religious strain, and 'Christmas Eve' and 'Easter Day' show the changed mind at work. When he speaks of not

[1] Letter of E. B. B. to R. B., August 15, 1846.

being a Christian we are inclined to think that it was because in Browning's estimation the person worthy to call himself by that name does not exist, and that he objected to the glib use of a misnomer. There is a hint of this attitude in some words of Guido in ' The Ring and the Book '[1]:

> I think I never was at any time
> A Christian, *as you nickname all the world.*

Browning's Christology is as sound and orthodox as it could possibly be. He believed that Christ was the unique and divine Son of God, differing from all other men not only in degree, but in kind ; that God was in Christ in this sense. He does not hesitate to call Christ God. We recall the last two lines of ' A Death in the Desert,' where, concerning the decease of St. John, he says :

> now the man
> Lies as he lay once, breast to breast with God.

This Christology is the central thing in Browning's religious faith, and for him it is the clue to the riddle of the universe. In the same poem he tells us :

> I say, the acknowledgement of God in Christ
> Accepted by the reason, solves for thee
> All questions in the earth and out of it.

Moreover, ' Christmas Eve ' and ' Easter Day' force us to conclude that he believed the idea there expressed that wherever love is manifested Christ is present, not in a merely metaphorical sense, but actually there is the presence of the Risen Lord, very man and very God. Christ, for Browning, is the incarnation of that principle of divine love which is ever at work in human

[1] Guido, 1916-17. Cf. also ' Holy Cross Day,' xviii. and xx.

lives, and in the light of which alone all the happenings of human life are explicable.

> For life, with all its yields of joy or woe
> And hope and fear—believe the agèd friend—
> Is just our chance o' the prize of learning love,
> How love might be, hath been indeed, and is.

'Literary criticism,' says Professor Dowden,[1] 'which would interpret Browning's meaning in any other sense may be ingenious, but it is not disinterested, and some side wind blows it far from the mark.'

This does not mean that Browning's whole scheme of Christian thought was in line with orthodox theology. It was not in the matter of his belief in hell, as we shall see. It was not in the matter of his belief in the Atonement, which by some is regarded as central. Indeed, it may be for this reason, rather than for the one given above, that Browning eschewed the name 'Christian.'[2] Probably Browning found it difficult to harmonize the then orthodox teaching about the Atonement—involving an angry God who demanded the death of Christ to expiate the sin of man and satisfy His 'eternal law of righteousness,' before He could forgive His own children—with his own conception of a God of Love; and he would give up anything that would ever seem to conflict with that great fundamental concept of his religious thinking. Without that conception the poet's whole universe would have utterly collapsed. He never misses any opportunity of emphasizing that God is Love, and that any other conception is unthinkable.

For him,

> the loving worm within its clod
> Were diviner than a loveless God
> Amid his worlds, I will dare to say.
> ('Christmas Eve.')

[1] *Life of Robert Browning*, p. 127.
[2] Browning disliked being tied to a creed. He said that 'religious certainties are required for the undeveloped mind, but a growing intelligence walks best by a receding light.'

For him, as he says in 'An Epistle of Karshish,' the 'All-Great' must be the 'All-loving' too; and

> There is no good of life but love—but love!
> What else looks good, is some shade flung from love;
> Love gilds it, gives it worth. Be warned by me,
> Never you cheat yourself one instant! Love,
> Give love, ask only love, and leave the rest!
> ('In a Balcony.')

Summarizing, then, we may say that we have in Browning a poet who is a profound student and lover of human souls, and whose work, especially after 1850, is strongly coloured by Christian sentiment. He may prefer not to label himself a Christian—and who could give a different answer from his to his questioner?—yet we have seen already that some of his fundamental conceptions can receive no other description. All this is bound to colour his treatment of a subject which is by nature religious and which concerns the destiny of the human soul.

4

There are three further preliminary considerations which we must carefully note, for they profoundly influence the poet's conception of the after-world. The first is his idea of the element of struggle as a necessary and welcome part of the soul's life and progress. The second is the conviction that nothing the nature of which is essentially good can ever be lost. The third is an emphasis on individuality.

(*a*) *The element of struggle as a necessary and welcome feature of the soul's progress.*—Robert Browning might almost have written words which Carlyle uses in writing of David in *Heroes and Hero Worship*[1]: Life 'may be struggle often baffled, sore baffled, down as into entire wreck, yet a struggle never ended; ever with tears, repentance, true unconquerable purpose,

[1] p. 43.

begun anew.' No easy virtue, easily reached, appealed to our poet. He makes a very unattractive picture of life in 'The Star of my God Rephan,' where is 'no want,' 'no change,' 'no growth,' where 'nothing begins,' where there are 'no winters,' 'no hope,' 'no fears,' and where we find 'all happy'; and he concludes:

> A Voice said, ' So wouldst thou strive, not rest ?
> Burn and not smoulder, win by worth,
> Not rest content with a wealth that's dearth ?
> Thou art past Rephan ; thy place be earth ! '

As we shall see later, he is not nearly so much at home in dealing with the human soul when his imagination can conceive for it no further necessity for any struggle. Indeed, a case can be made out that his conception of the after-world is characterized by the idea of incessant struggle. He most certainly would have subscribed to the dictum of Robert Louis Stevenson that ' to travel hopefully is better than to arrive, and true success is to labour.' His last word for the human soul, we think, is the word success. But he is far more interested in the penultimate word, and that is failure. He loves to picture the soul which scarcely attains, which in the judgement of the world perhaps does not attain, and yet which wins through at last, or whose failure is itself a victory of the soul. His happy warrior was

> One who never turned his back but marched breast forward,
> Never doubted clouds would break,
> Never dreamed, though right were worsted, wrong would triumph ;
> Held we fall to rise, are baffled to fight better,
>   Sleep to wake.
>   (Epilogue to 'Asolando.')

Obviously such a philosophy solves many problems. Evil is not so much a positive entity. It is rather the negation of good.[1] It is a space in the fabric of life which will be filled up later.

> The evil is null, is naught, is silence implying sound;
> What was good shall be good, with, for evil, so much good
>   more.
> ('Abt Vogler.')

Ignorance is not a maddening infirmity, as Paracelsus thought even up to his very death-bed. It should be recognized as evidence of the capabilities of growth for the intellect in the future. All man's limitations are such evidences, and they are there so that by conflict with them man's soul may develop and grow. This philosophy seems to us to imply belief in immortality. Man does not reach perfection at death, and his imperfection implies a life in which perfection may be reached. Man's soul cannot in this life get the full benefit of the battle—since the body handicaps its possibilities—or full compensation for life's injustices. So says Festus:

>   It is our trust
> That there is yet another world to mend
> All error and mischance.
> ('Paracelsus.')

This is a doctrine of hope based on the imperfection of this life which runs through the whole of 'Paracelsus,' and we think it is sound. And, though we have quoted a poem essentially dramatic, there is confirmatory evidence elsewhere.

> 'Tis a lifelong toil till our lump be leaven—
> The better! What's come to perfection perishes.
> Things learned on earth, we shall practise in heaven.[2]
> ('Old Pictures in Florence.')

The whole poem, one imagines, was written to show the

---

[1] Evil *appears* to man in this life to be a very real foe, so that he may have the strength of soul only attainable through strife. Cf. Professor Herford, *Robert Browning*, p. 299.

[2] The same idea runs through the poem 'Cleon.'

hope based on deficiency, given the will to struggle towards the goal.

Morality always appears to Browning in the form of a struggle. The sin without forgiveness, to him, is indifference and spiritual languor; ' the unlit lamp, and the ungirt loin.'[1]

> No, when the fight begins within himself,
> A man's worth something. God stoops o'er his head,
> Satan looks up between his feet—both tug—
> He's left, himself, i' the middle: the soul wakes
> And grows. Prolong that battle through his life!
> Never leave growing till the life to come.
> ('Bishop Blougram's Apology.')

> Let a man contend to the uttermost
> For his life's set prize, be it what it will!
> ('The Statue and the Bust.')

Even Pompilia, the most gentle, may we not say the most beautiful, character in the whole of the English poetry of the century, whom the Pope calls

> My flower,
> My rose, I gather for the breast of God?—

even she recognizes the element of struggle:

> a worm must turn
> If it would have its wrong observed by God.
> I did spring up, attempt to thrust aside
> That ice-block 'twixt the sun and me, lay low
> The neutralizer of all good and truth.
> ('Pompilia,' 1591–5.)

We may content ourselves with one last quotation from ' Rabbi Ben Ezra ' (vi.) :

Then, welcome each rebuff
That turns earth's smoothness rough,
Each sting that bids nor sit nor stand but go!
Be our joy three parts pain!
Strive, and hold cheap the strain;
Learn, nor account the pang; dare, never grudge the throe!

[1] 'The Statue and the Bust.'

As Professor Herford says, ' The best commentary on Browning's faith is the saying of Meredith, " The fact that character can be and is developed by the clash of circumstances is to me a warrant for infinite hope." '[1]

(b) *The conviction that nothing good can ever be lost.*—This is another principle which runs through Browning's work, and which is obviously going to have a great bearing on his treatment of the idea of immortality. Ultimately it brings him to accept the theory of universalism, since there is indestructible good in all men. We have seen this as we looked into Browning's mind when he viewed the corpses in the Morgue at Paris. We find the same sentiment in ' Paracelsus ' :

> Be sure that God
> Ne'er dooms to waste the strength he deigns impart.

In ' Abt Vogler ' we get this principle expressed with a passion and fervour—perhaps one should add with a dogmatism—nowhere else equalled in the whole of Browning's work :

There shall never be one lost good ! . . .
. . . .
All we have willed or hoped or dreamed of good shall exist ;
Not its semblance, but itself ; no beauty, nor good, nor power
Whose voice had gone forth, but each survives for the melodist
When eternity affirms the conception of an hour.

(c) *The conviction of the importance of the individual soul.*—One of the supreme convictions of Browning, a conviction which influenced all his work, was that of the individuality of man, the infinite value of the human personality. His use of the dramatic monologue shows this. As our mind is allowed to ponder over Browning's poems, how vividly stand out the portraits of Pippa, Paracelsus, Pompilia, and the rest !

[1] Professor Herford, *Robert Browning* p. 168.

There is a loneliness about them which is significant of Browning's lack of interest in the humanity of the crowd and his love for people as individuals.

So it comes about that the individual is of infinite worth to God. We recall the lines in ' Fifine at the Fair ' :

> Partake my confidence ! No creature's made so mean
> But that, some way, it boasts, could we investigate,
> Its supreme worth.

Browning rejected pantheism. There are passages which could be quoted to show a certain tendency of mind towards it ; but he always breaks off before it is reached. God is not an absentee from the universe, but neither is He a pervading Spirit within it.

As there was a demarcation between God and nature, so is there always a demarcation between God and man. God and man may have intimate communion ; but the distinctiveness of the one is never lost in the other. Browning believes in the divineness of the universe ; but with this belief he holds, most tenaciously, the individuality of man :

> From first to last of lodging, I was I.[1]

Obviously this conviction is going to play an important part in the poet's view of an after-life.

5

If these findings have any value, we realize that no one who held them could possibly believe that death is the end of all things for the human spirit. During the last years of his life Browning scorned such an idea. ' Death, death,' he broke out on one occasion, ' it is this harping on death that I despise so much. In fiction, in poetry, French as well as English, and, I am told, in America also, in art, in literature, the shadow of death, call it what you will, despair, negation, indifference is upon us. But what fools who talk thus ! Why,

[1] ' Prince Hohenstiel-Schwangau.'

amico mio, you know as well as I, that death is life ; just as our daily momentarily dying body is none the less alive, and ever recruiting new forces of existence. Without death, which is our churchyardy crape-like word for change, for growth, there could be no prolongation of that which we call life. Never say of me that I am dead.'[1] In conversation with Mr. Rudolph Lehmann, an artist, he said concerning a future life, ' I have doubted and denied it, and I fear have even printed my doubts ; but now I am as deeply convinced that there is something after death. If you ask me what, I no more know it than my dog knows who and what I am. He knows that I am there and that is enough for him.'[2]

The soul, doubtless, is immortal—where a soul can be discerned.

Yours, for instance : you know physics, something of geology,
Mathematics are your pastime ; souls shall rise in their degree ;
Butterflies may dread extinction,—you'll not die, it cannot be !
(' A Toccata of Galuppi's.')

Thus sings the dying Paracelsus :

    And this is death : I understand it all.
      New being waits me ; new perceptions must
    Be born in me before I plunge therein ;
      Which last is Death's affair ; and while I speak
    Minute by minute he is filling me
      With power ; *and while my foot is on the threshold
Of boundless life* . . .
      I turn new knowledge upon old events,
    And the effect is . . . but I must not tell.

    . . . .
                    If I stoop
Into a dark, tremendous sea of cloud,
It is but for a time ; I press God's lamp
Close to my breast ; its splendour, soon or late,
Will pierce the gloom : I shall emerge one day.

[1] Quoted by Chesterton, *Robert Browning*, p. 130.
[2] Quoted by Dowden, *Life of Robert Browning*, p. 326.

The poem which Browning devotes wholly to the question whether death is the extinction of the human soul is ' La Saisiaz,' though his conceptions of immortality do not rise to their high-water mark in this poem. 'La Saisiaz' (The Sun) was the name of a villa up in the Savoy Alps near Geneva where Browning, with his sister and a friend, called Miss Edgerton-Smith, spent part of the summer of 1877. The latter was preparing for a mountain excursion with the two former when she suddenly died of heart disease on the morning of September 14. Browning afterwards climbed alone to the summit of Salève, the mountain behind the villa, and the poem was born from the thoughts and emotions of this lonely climb, accomplished at the age of sixty-six :

> what seemed You have we consigned
> Peacefully to—what I think were, of all earth-beds, to your mind
> Most the choice for quiet, yonder :
> . . . . . .
> Climbing,—here I stand : but You—where?

The poem is Browning's debate with himself on the question of immortality ; but it is saved from an undue preponderance of the didactic because it is born of a poignant emotional experience, and is shot through and through with that insight which is the very fabric of which poetry is made. The poet does not take either a Christian or a non-Christian attitude here. He left on one side the question of the Christian revelation. He rather rests his argument on a rational basis acceptable either to a thinker who did or to one who did not accept the authority of revealed religion. We must not take the poem as manifesting any definite attitude to Christianity, because this was not the poet's purpose. He wants to answer the question without taking anything for granted, and to arrive at what is *for him the truth*, whatever the cost in sacrificing preconceived notions and lifelong desires.

The first part of the poem is an assertion of certain facts—the fact of himself, and the fact of the Cause of himself, which, for the moment, he will call God:

> the thing itself which questions, answers—*is*, it knows,
> As it also knows the thing perceived outside itself, a force
> Actual ere its own beginning, operative through its course,
> Unaffected by its end . . .
> Call this—God, then, call that—soul, and both—the only
>   facts for me.

If this life be all, then all he can say is that it is doubtful whether it derives from a source supreme in goodness, wisdom, and power, since for his own part sorrow preponderates over joy. Given that the universe is not mere chance, the only hypothesis by which it can be regarded as the result of a beneficent intelligence is that this life is a probation for another. Earth is

> a pupil's place,
> And life, time—with all their chances, changes—just probation-
>   space.

If this hypothesis be accepted it is seen to *work*, and make sense.

> Only grant a second life, I acquiesce
> In this present life as failure, count misfortune's worst assaults
> Triumph, not defeat, assured that loss so much the more
>   exalts
> Gain about to be.

In this way ignorance, ugliness, evil, and falsehood are themselves evidences of future knowledge, beauty, goodness, and truth. So injustice, pain, imperfection, incompletion, and failure argue a life when justice, happiness, perfection, completion, and success shall be won.

> Knowledge means
> Ever-renewed assurance by defeat
> That victory is somehow still to reach.
>   ('A Pillar at Sebzevar.')

Or, again, in the poem under discussion ('La Saisiaz'),
Take the joys and bear the sorrows—neither with extreme concern!
Living here means nescience simply: 'tis next life that helps to learn.

. . . .

Bravely bustle through thy being . . .
. . . Soon shall things be unperplexed,
And the right and wrong, now tangled, lie unravelled in the next.

The same idea is in 'Abt Vogler':
what is our failure here but a triumph's evidence
For the fullness of the days? Have we withered or agonized?
Why else was the pause prolonged but that singing might issue thence?
Why rushed the discords in but that harmony should be prized?

And again in the words of the Pope in 'The Ring and the Book' (1374-80):
still faith stands:
I can believe this dread machinery
Of sin and sorrow, would confound me else,
Devised,—all pain, at most expenditure
Of pain by Who devised pain,—to evolve,
By new machinery in counterpart,
The moral qualities of man—how else?

Yet the poet emphasizes that all we must expect concerning a life beyond the grave is a hope. For if certainty be given us, then earth ceases to be a place of probation. If we possessed the certainty of a future life we should not be content patiently to educate our souls in this. And if that life were fully revealed, so much the more discontented should we become with this.

o'er our heaven again cloud closes, until, lo—
Hope the arrowy, just as constant, comes to pierce its gloom, compelled
By a power and by a purpose which, if no one else beheld,
I behold in life, so—hope!

In the latter part of the poem we have a dialogue which is a duel between thrusting Fancy and parrying

Reason. Fancy is the spontaneous self; Reason is the judicial self. Mere emotional conjecture, the effect of the beauty of nature, the mere opinions of men, the thought that God would necessarily be unjust and man necessarily wronged if immortality were a lie—these considerations are scrutinized with acid severity. The end of the matter is a hope, strongly supported by reason, in the immortality of the soul.

The poem in which Browning deals most fully with the question of immortality does not show us Browning at his best as a poet. We could wish that he had written his thoughts on immortality in the mood in which he wrote the lines beginning

> O lyric Love, half angel and half bird.

What we do find in 'La Saisiaz' is the calm deliberation of the poet concerning death and the hereafter, and a grouping of many ideas on the subject which are scattered throughout his earlier work.

We see, then, that Browning accepts the idea of another life following this, for which this is a probation. We also observe how his conception, previously noted, of life as a struggle in which character is beaten out, and the view that nothing good is ever lost, contribute to, and fit in with, his idea of probation, making, as far as we have gone, a harmonious system of thought.

The soul has a 'life allotment,'

> wherein, by hypothesis
> Soul is bound to pass probation, prove its powers, and exercise
> Sense and thought on fact;

and

> Just so certainly depends it on the use to which man turns
> Earth, the good and evil done there, whether after death he earns
> Life eternal,—heaven, the phrase be, or eternal death,— say, hell.
> As his deeds, so proves his portion, doing ill or doing well.
>
> ('La Saisiaz.')

'What were life?' asks Gerald de Lairesse:

> Did soul stand still therein, forgo her strife
> Through the ambiguous Present to the goal
> Of some all-reconciling Future? Soul,
> Nothing has been which shall not bettered be
> Hereafter.
>
> (xiii.)

The Pope voices the same thought in 'The Ring and the Book' (1411 ff.):

> This life is training and a passage;
> . . . .
> The moral sense grows but by exercise.
> 'Tis even as man grew probatively
> Initiated in Godship, set to make
> A fairer moral world than this he finds,
> Guess now what shall be known hereafter.
> . . . .
> Life is probation and the earth no goal
> But starting-point of man: compel him strive.

This view of our present life as probation must not be understood to imply that we should hurry through it in any ascetic sense, giving it no value in itself, and depriving ourselves of the elements of happiness which it was meant to contain for us.

> This world's no blot for us,
> Nor blank; it means intensely, and means good:
> To find its meaning is my meat and drink.
>
> Have you found your life distasteful?
> My life did, and does, smack sweet.
> . . . .
> I find earth not grey but rosy,
> Heaven not grim but fair of hue.
> Do I stoop? I pluck a posy.
> Do I stand and stare? All's blue.
>
> ('At the Mermaid.')

There is no unworthy other-worldliness about our poet.

6

It is interesting and relevant to our quest to ask what Browning thinks of the human body. The orthodoxy of his day held a belief in the actual resurrection of the flesh after death; that is, the actual emergence from the grave of the same particles of which the body was formed in this life. The preceding essays illustrate the fact that no other poets of the century believed this. Nor does Browning, though he boldly speaks, in some of his poems, of a soul as though it were still garbed in the flesh—'Evelyn Hope,' for example; but this does not mean that he believes in the actual ' resurrection of the flesh.' One is bound to use language which implies some kind of embodiment of the spirit, just as our language about God is bound to some extent to be anthropomorphic, though we believe that God is Spirit.

An indication of Browning's true thought on this matter may be accurately judged from an incident in his life. When his wife died he took measures to see that her grave was kept decently; but he never felt any sentiment regarding the mere body of the one who had been more than life itself to him for more than sixteen years. Mrs. Orr[1] says, ' For him, a body from which the soul had passed held nothing of the person whose earthly vesture it had been. He had no sympathy for the still human tenderness with which so many of us regard the mortal remains of those we have loved. . . . He would claim all respect for the corpse, but he would turn away from it.' Writing to Mr. George Moulton-Barrett, in October 1866, he says, ' I have no kind of concern as to where the old clothes of myself shall be thrown.'

This is the view which, in the main, is expressed in his poems. The body is like an old suit of clothes, which one lays down when it is outworn; or it is a

---

[1] Mrs. Sutherland Orr, *Life and Letters of Robert Browning*, p. 243.

prison from which one escapes with joy into a life of greater liberty and untramelled freedom and scope.

> See this soul of ours !
> How it strives weakly in the child, is loosed
> In manhood, clogged by sickness, back compelled
> By age and waste, set free at last by death.
> ('Paracelsus.')

Or again in the same poem :

> There is an inmost centre in us all,
> Where truth abides in fullness ; and around,
> Wall upon wall, the gross flesh hems it in,
> This perfect, clear perception—which is truth.
> A baffling and perverting carnal mesh
> Binds it, and makes all error.

Reason, in ' La Saisiaz,' says,

Life to come will be an improvement on the life that's now ; destroy
Body's thwartings, there's no longer screen betwixt soul and soul's joy.

And we have the same idea in ' Reverie.'

Sometimes the figure is changed to that of a bandage or a veil. Both terms are used of the body in ' Balaustion's Adventure.' St. John (in 'A Death in the Desert') has almost done with the body. There is ' scarce a shred between ' himself and the light of the heavenly vision. Something of that vision penetrates to him, the bandage growing thin ; but youth in the heyday of physical health cannot see it, nor can the aged saint unbind the eyes of youth and give them sight.

> And how shall I assure them ? Can they share
> —They who have flesh, a veil of youth and strength
> About each spirit, that needs must bide its time,
> Living and learning still as years assist
> Which wear the thickness thin, and let man see,—
> With me who hardly am withheld at all ?

Sometimes the figure changes to that of a room through which the spirit passes on to a further existence, but the meaning is the same. He speaks in 'Abt Vogler' of

> the wonderful dead, who have passed through the body and gone.

Yet there is no disparagement of the body. Browning does not appear to hold the ancient heresy of the essential evil of the flesh. The soul seems so to outshine and outsoar the body that the latter seems evil. But it is only by comparison. And indeed a man would still be a brute if his body kept pace with his soul. The highest test of the body is the extent to which it can help the soul, on the latter's lonely way.

> What is he but a brute
> Whose flesh has soul to suit,
> Whose spirit works lest arms and legs want play?
> To man, propose this test—
> Thy body at its best,
> How far can that project thy soul on its long way?
> ('Rabbi Ben Ezra.')

Nor must man label as evil what is the design of God. And indeed life in the flesh is pleasant, and need not hold back the development of the soul any more than the attitude of the soul need arrest physical fitness.

> Perfect I call Thy plan:
> Thanks that I was a man!
> Maker, remake, complete,—I trust what Thou shalt do.

> For pleasant is this flesh;
> Our soul in its rose-mesh,
> Pulled ever to the earth, still yearns for rest;
> . . . .
> Let us not always say,
> 'Spite of this flesh to-day
> I strove, made head, gained ground upon the whole!'

> As the bird wings and sings,
> Let us cry, ' All good things
> Are ours, nor soul helps flesh more, now, than flesh helps soul!'

And, again, in 'A Death in the Desert':

> . . . See the double way wherein we are led,
> How the soul learns diversely from the flesh!
> With flesh, that hath so little time to stay,
> And yields mere basement for the soul's emprise.

Nor does the flesh wholly obscure beauty of mind. In part it reveals it.

> the flesh that claimed
> Unduly my regard, she thought, the taste, she blamed
> In me, for things extern, was all mistake, she finds,
> Or will find, when I prove that bodies show me minds,
> That, through the outward sign, the inward grace allures,
> And sparks from heaven transpierce earth's coarsest
>   covertures.
>   ('Fifine at the Fair.')

Though the body is likened to a prison, Browning does not mean that metaphor to be pressed too far. He knows well enough those moments when the spirit leans out of the window of the body; moments, perhaps, when it escapes; certainly moments when one spirit seems actually to mingle with another.

> We knew that a bar was broken between
> Life and life: we were mixed at last
> In spite of the mortal screen.

7

Our preliminary considerations led us to anticipate that, for Browning, progress and growth are necessary functions for the soul of man, whether in this life or the next. The soul that emerges is the same soul.

> From first to last of lodging, I was I,
> And not at all the place that harbour'd me;

and it is natural to suppose that the soul carries with it

the same characteristics. So we hear Pompilia cry (1786),

> O lover of my life, O soldier saint,
> No work begun shall ever pause for death;

and that seems to be Browning's view not only concerning love, but concerning all worthy activities of the human spirit. Life spells growth. Growth means progress. So, though in 'Old Pictures in Florence' we have the lines—

> There remaineth a rest for the people of God:
> And I have had troubles enough, for one—

yet they are merely part of the appropriate dramatic setting. Far more typical is the passage in the same poem in which he tends to the

> fancy some lean to and others hate—
> That, when this life is ended, begins
> New work for the soul in another state.
> (xxi.)

There is just a possible hint in Browning of the idea which we noted in Tennyson of future existences in other worlds. Yet we cannot attach importance to it, for we dare not say that a casual reference in words used by a dramatic figure express the mind of Browning.[1]

Says Evelyn Hope's lover:

> I claim you still, for my one love's sake!
> Delayed it may be for more lives yet,
> Through worlds I shall traverse, not a few:
> Much is to learn, much to forget
> Ere the time be come for taking you.
> (iv.)

For ourselves, we believe this simply to mean a period of purification for the soul on the other side; but

[1] It is to avoid this error that I have rather overburdened the chapter with numerous passages illustrating each idea. Browning, the poet, and a character in a poem, may be three distinct people, with differing ideas.

there is no doubt about Browning's conviction that progress is to continue after death, for the idea is repeated again and again. He rejoices

>   that man is hurled
>   From change to change unceasingly,
>   His soul's wings never furled.

Age may give man temporary rest, but soon there will come the call to new adventure.

>   And I shall thereupon
>   Take rest, ere I begone
>   Once more on my adventure brave and new:
>   Fearless and unperplexed,
>   When I wage battle next,
>   What weapons to select, what armour to indue.
>   ('Rabbi Ben Ezra.')

The Grammarian portrayed in 'A Grammarian's Funeral' believed in progress hereafter.

> This man said rather, 'Actual life comes next?
>   Patience a moment! . . .'
>   .   .   .   .
> Others mistrust and say, 'But time escapes:
>   Live now or never!'
> He said, 'What's time? Leave Now for dogs and apes!
>   Man has Forever.'

And in 'One Word More,' dedicated to his wife, he regrets that he cannot paint pictures for her, or carve statues, or express himself adequately in music. His only attainment is to write her verse; but in other lives he may be able, because of the progress of his soul, to shower upon her all the gifts which love would fain give love:

>   I shall never, in the years remaining,
>   Paint you pictures, no, nor carve you statues,
>   Make you music that should all-express me;
>   So it seems: I stand on my attainment.

> This of verse alone, one life allows me;
> Verse and nothing else have I to give you.
> *Other heights in other lives, God willing :*
> All the gifts from all the heights, your own, Love!

So one feels that Browning would find heaven enough in constant exploration of new possibilities stretching before his eager spirit and awaiting conquest, especially if his loved one shared the quest, and

> heaven just prove that I and she
> Ride, ride together, for ever ride?
> ('The Last Ride Together.')

The last words we have from Browning's pen are a kind of challenge onward. There is not much expectation of relaxation in the mind of the aged warrior. He cried,

> Greet the unseen with a cheer!
> Bid him forward, breast and back as either should be,
> 'Strive and thrive!' cry 'Speed—fight on, fare ever
> There as here.'
> (Epilogue to 'Asolando.')

8

We desire to ask, however, what Browning conceives to be the aim and purpose of all this striving. Did his mind really rest in the idea of an eternity of effort? Many would answer this question in the affirmative, and without doubt it is a plausible position. Browning, we agree, was not concerned about the goal of human effort. To him an eternal striving was goal enough. So high a value does he place on conflict and its resulting progress that, as Professor Herford says,[1] ' Progress was too deeply ingrained in Browning's conception of what was ultimately good, and therefore ultimately real, not to find entrance into his heaven, were it only by some casual back-door of involuntary intuition.'

[1] *Robert Browning*, p. 293.

Conflict, in his view, certainly does persist in the next life to some extent and for some period. In 'Prospice' he says that, though at death

> the journey is done, and the summit attained,
> And the barriers fall;

yet still

> a battle's to fight ere the guerdon be gained,
> The reward of it all.

But he hesitates to tell us what the reward of it all is. He shrinks from triumph, because he feels it would be marred by memories of a struggle more precious and valuable than victory. He shrinks from the contemplation of the accomplished deed, because it is less in his eyes than the doing. The tang of striving is absent in the achievement.

> Thus old memories mar the actual triumph;
> Thus the doing savours of disrelish;
> Thus achievement lacks a gracious somewhat.
> ('One Word More,' ix.)

What is the goal for Browning? Tennyson spoke of

> One far-off divine event,
> To which the whole creation moves,

and we surmised that for him this was the gathering in of all souls into a state of harmony with the Divine Mind and Will. It is worth our while and relevant to our subject to note that Browning also accepts this position, though we think, as we shall show later, his mind did not rest there. But in theological language Browning is an undoubted universalist. He never will allow that a soul created by God ever passes out into the darkness, whether we regard that darkness as the extinction or annihilation of the soul or whether we regard it as the endless punishment of the wicked.

Here again, very characteristically, Browning will allow a soul to be all but annihilated. Annihilation is the last word but one. We note the 'wellnigh' in the words of Paracelsus:

> No mean trick
> He left untried, and truly wellnigh wormed
> All traces of God's finger out of him:
> Then died, grown old.

In 'The Ring and the Book' Caponsacchi sees Guido sinking lower and lower:

> Not to die so much as slide out of life,
> Pushed by the general horror and common hate
> Low, lower,—left o' the very ledge of things
> I seem to see him catch convulsively,
> One by one at all honest forms of life,
> At reason, order, decency, and use—
> To cramp him and get foothold by at least;
> And still they disengage them from his clutch.
> . . . . .
> And thus I see him slowly and surely edged
> Off all the tableland where life upsprings,
> Aspiring to be immortality,

until poor Guido is left

> At the horizontal line, creation's verge,
> From what just is to absolute nothingness.
>   (Caponsacchi, 1911 ff.)

Guido himself is pathetically willing to be annihilated. He says,

> What shall I say to God?
> This, if I find the tongue and keep the mind—
> 'Do Thou wipe out the being of me, and smear
> This soul from off Thy white of things, I blot!
> I am one huge and sheer mistake.'
>   (Guido, 935-9.)

But Guido does not pass over 'the horizontal line. One may perhaps hear Browning himself in the Pope's 'which must not be.' For if Guido has to be annihilated or even perpetually damned, then God has failed, and that 'must not be.' In a wonderful passage the Pope says,

> So may the truth be flashed out by one blow,
> And Guido see, one instant, and be saved.
> Else I avert my face, nor follow him
> Into that sad obscure sequestered state
> Where God unmakes but to remake the soul
> He else made first in vain; which must not be.

Here we see further evidence of our preliminary principle that nothing good can ever be lost; and Browning would add that when, in human judgement, the fires of the soul have been utterly quenched, God may see a spark, which, fanned into a blaze, may kindle the whole being once again.

Beneath the veriest ash, there hides a spark of soul
Which, quickened by love's breath, may yet pervade the whole
O' the grey, and, free again, be fire?
('Fifine at the Fair.')

> What began best can't end worst,

he tells us in a passage already quoted; and the multitudinous ways open to the infinite Love—always in Browning a synonym for God—mean for the poet that *some* way will always be found to win back the soul to harmony with the Divine.

> I exult
> That God, by God's ways occult,
> May—doth, I will believe—bring back
> All wanderers to a single track.
> ('Christmas Eve,' **xx**.)

As he rejects annihilation and absorption as the ultimate goal for any soul, so he rejects also the idea of an endless hell. The idea of suffering viewed as retribution he rejected, as we shall see. The idea of a punishment indefinitely prolonged he saw to be a contradiction in terms, for every form of punishment points to its own negation. It only exists in order to prepare for the time when it shall not be needed. As he says in another connexion,

> Why, the child grown man, you burn the rod.
> ('Old Pictures in Florence.')

And, since we shall always be rational, it is relevant to argue from our idea of punishment here. There can be no value or relevance in a punishment which our own highest judgement deems unjust and absurd. The only value of post-death suffering is its purifying nature.

Browning's idea of hell is, I think, found in his lines about

> that sad, obscure, sequestered state,
> Where God unmakes, but to remake, the soul.

He thus conserves the only valuable element in the idea of purgatory. Let the figure of fire be preserved! But let us understand by it a fire which is not useless torture or endless retribution, but the burning away of the ' wood, hay, and stubble,' so that the hidden gold may be revealed and all that fire can consume be burnt away as unnecessary accretion.[1] So Guido thinks he will be

> Unmanned, remanned : I hold it probable—
> With something changeless at the heart of me
> To know me by, some nucleus that's myself :
> Accretions did it wrong ? Away with them—
> You soon shall see the use of fire!
> (Guido, 2393-7.)

[1] Cf. 1 Cor. iii. 11-15.

THE AFTER-WORLD OF THE POETS

In ' The Inn Album ' there is a very bitter and passionate exposure of the vulgar and superstitious doctrine of hell, which a narrow-minded clergyman ' dosed his flock withal ' :

>   Hell he made explicit. After death,
> Life : man created new, ingeniously
> Perfect for a vindictive purpose now
> That man, first fashioned in beneficence,
> Was proved a failure ; intellect at length
> Replacing old obtuseness, memory
> Made mindful of delinquent's bygone deeds
> Now that remorse was vain, which lifelong lay
> Dormant when lesson might be laid to heart ;
> New gift of observation up and down
> And round man's self, new power to apprehend
> Each necessary consequence of act
> In man for well or ill—things obsolete—
> Just granted to supplant the idiocy
> Man's only guide while act was yet to choose,
> With ill or well momentously its fruit ;
> A faculty of immense suffering
> Conferred on mind and body,—mind, erewhile
> Unvisited by one compunctious dream
> During sin's drunken slumber, startled up,
> Stung through and through by sin's significance
> Now that the holy was abolished—just
> As body which, alive, broke down beneath
> Knowledge, lay helpless in the path to good,
> Failed to accomplish aught legitimate,
> Achieve aught worthy—which grew old in youth,
> And at its longest fell a cut-down flower,—
> Dying, this too revived by miracle
> To bear no end of burthen, now that back
> Supported torture to no use at all,
> And live imperishably potent—since
> Life's potency was impotent to ward
> One plague off which made earth a hell before.

We fancy that it is Browning's own voice which we

hear in the comment which follows, and which says that such a doctrine was one

> which one healthy view of things,
> One sane sight of the general ordinance—
> Nature,—and its particular object,—man,—
> Which one mere eye-cast at the character
> Of Who made these and gave man sense to boot,
> Had dissipated once and evermore.

Browning can make sense of pain regarded as an educative factor of the soul's experience, but not as a retributive factor. Apart from being horrible and useless, the idea of such retribution is unintelligent and senseless; and Browning points out that to imagine that God is the kind of Person who acts in a way the worst man ever made would scorn—or run the risk of jail or the lunatic asylum—is absurd.

> A camel-driver, when his beast will bite,
> Thumps her athwart the muzzle: why?

His purpose is to teach the camel that mouths are for munching, not biting. But suppose

> He saw into the biter's very soul,
> And knew the fault was so repented of
> It could not happen twice?

Even then a blow is justified. The nature of the blow is changed. It is not retribution, but a friendly discipline. Moreover, it has a use in teaching other camels:

> Those long-necked sisters, see,
> Lean all a-stretch to know if biting meets
> Punishment or enjoys impunity.

But what of the camel-driver, who, when the journey is ended and the camel safe stabled, burns to

> avenge a wrong
> Suffered from six months since,

which, at the time was treated with indifference, possibly with approval? What if the driver thrust red-hot prongs into the soft parts of the camel's body, and left them there to hiss? This would be an outrage in man. And God cannot act less worthily than man.

Hell is not so much, Browning argues, that punishment is inflicted from without. It is remorse from within. As a child the poet threw into the fire a valuable book which belonged to his parents. He says,

> I grieve now at my loss by witlessness,
> But guilt was none to punish.

That which hurts is that later he deliberately of his own will turned from what he knew to be his father's wishes. The memories of these deeds

> Rankle like fire. Forgiveness? rather grant
> Forgetfulness! The past is past and lost.
> However near I stand in his regard,
> So much the nearer had I stood by steps
> Offered the feet which rashly spurned their help.
> That I call Hell; why further punishment?
> ('A Camel Driver.')

To have grieved the infinite Love on the one hand and to have done injury to one's soul on the other are the elements which make an inward remorse more galling and scorching than any outward flame. In this sense

> heaven or hell depend upon man's earthly deed.
> ('La Saisiaz.')

9

Though Browning will not allow either annihilation or endless torment to be the last word for any human soul, we do not think that this universalism is the ultimate goal in his mind for humanity. We have seen that he believes that all souls will be gathered in so as to complete God's family at long last. But we believe that his thought is that even this climax is but another penultimate word ; that that state itself is a kind of second infancy of the race leading to yet higher realms of being. In this way he can prolong the period of struggle yet again. We believe—though in all the books on Browning, with one possible exception, to be mentioned later, the present writer has not seen this view stated—that the poet's ultimate conception of the destiny of the human race was that man should become divine. Not that man should become God, either equal with God or absorbed into God ; but that manhood should be so raised to its highest power that it could only be called godhead ; humanity so lifted up by aeons of struggle and growth to become something only to be described as divinity ; just as man to-day has so developed physically from his simian ancestors that he cannot now be adequately described as ape-like.

All through his works Browning emphasizes the *divine element* in man. The germ of a divine life within humanity is one of his favourite themes. We believe—and we shall quote evidence later—that, scarcely daring to make the thought articulate, Browning's speculative mind saw that there is something dissatisfying in the idea of endless struggle, and that the only other satisfactory ultimate was godhood. Men shall be as gods.

This thought, though daring, is not, of course, new. It was Athanasius who said, ' Filius Dei efficitur filius hominis, ut filios hominum faceret filios Dei.' Moreover, if pantheistic absorption be avoided on the one hand—and a Western mind like Browning's would eschew this, though an Eastern mind can view with complacency the loss of personality—and the disruption of the eternal unity be avoided on the other, then it is hard to imagine the ultimate destiny of man as other than a species of god; that is, a being so developed above what man is now that it would be as inadequate to call that lofty being man as it would be now to call man a brute, even though the difference be achieved in both cases by gradual growth and development, not by a miraculous change of nature.

Such a conception is no kind of return to the polytheism from which we have progressed : firstly, because no claim is being made that man becomes equal with God or worthy of worship; but secondly, and more cogently, because the suggestion made concerns the ultimate life in some consummation of the ages when all life which is human shall have passed beyond the limitations of the flesh (as definitely as all man-becoming apes have now passed from the simian stage) and not only *entered* a spirit world, but passed through a further period of struggle and growth on the other side.

We have called this latter period a kind of second infancy of the race, and we think Browning deals with this view in ' Paracelsus ' :

> progress is
> The law of life, man is not Man as yet.
> Nor shall I deem his object served, his end
> Attained, his genuine strength put fairly forth,
> While only here and there a star dispels
> The darkness, here and there a towering mind
> O'erlooks its prostrate fellows : when the host
> Is out at once to the despair of night,
> When all mankind alike is perfected,
> Equal in full-blown powers—then, not till then,
> I say, *begins man's general infancy.*

That is to say, when man has reached perfection, which he will do, not as an individual, but as a race, then he will begin a further stage, and reach his second objective after his second infancy in the same way.

Man will certainly never be content to set limits to his ambition. Browning's emphasis on struggle evidences this point, and, unless we have to say there is no limit, then the only rational limit is complete knowledge and power.

Such a position is not out of harmony with the religious approach to philosophy. We may note that in Greek, Roman, and Norse mythology men and women are constantly rewarded by being made gods and goddesses by Zeus, Jupiter, or Odin. In Hinduism man's highest goal is the avoidance of future reincarnations and absorption into the Deity. In Buddhism Nirvana is the goal of all existence. In Confucianism and Taoism the mortal attains to such a heavenly condition that he is regarded as worthy of the worship of his descendants. In Christianity the idea is not absent. Paul speaks of men as 'joint heirs with Christ.'[1] The author of the Second Epistle of Peter speaks of men as ' partakers of the Divine Nature.'[2] The seer of Patmos makes our Lord say that to him that overcometh shall be given to sit down on His throne, ' even as I overcame and sat down with My Father on His throne '[3]; and the author of the Fourth Gospel makes Christ speak of the glory that he had with God before the world was, and pray that His followers ' may be one as we are.'[4] Doubtful as these evidences are for the Christian postion, they are cumulatively forceful. We may ask whether the whole purpose of the Incarnation was not to show the possibility of the godhood—as yet potential—of man.

We must now turn and ask if this can be regarded as Browning's view. We are aware of the danger of supposing that Browning speaks through his dramatic characters. Therefore we must collect a number of instances of this view before we can claim it as his. We believe, however, that he does often speak through the

---

[1] Rom. viii. 17.
[2] 2 Pet. i. 4.
[3] Rev. iii. 21.
[4] John xvii. 5, 11.

Pope in ' The Ring and the Book.' Then consider the following lines (1373–84) :

> I reach into the dark,
> Feel what I cannot see, and still faith stands:
> I can believe this dread machinery
> Of sin and sorrow, would confound me else,
> Devised,—all pain, at most expenditure
> Of pain by Who devised pain,—to evolve,
> By new machinery in counterpart,
> The moral qualities of man—how else ?—
> To make him love in turn and be beloved,
> Creative and self-sacrificing too,
> *And thus eventually God-like (ay,*
> ' *I have said ye are Gods'—shall it be said for naught ?*)

Then, turning to ' Paracelsus,' we find these lines : God

> dwells in all,
> From life's minute beginnings, up at last
> To man—the consummation of this scheme
> Of being, the completion of this sphere
> Of life. . . .
> . . . .
> And, man produced, all has its end thus far:
> *But in completed man begins anew*
> *A tendency to God.*

If we turn to ' Prince Hohenstiel-Schwangau,' we find the lines :

> God, perchance,
> Grants each new man, by some as new a mode,
> Intercommunication with Himself,
> Wreaking on finiteness infinitude.

Support of our point occurs in a passage later on in the same poem, which, though we have to present it torn from its context, and though it is an example of poetic mysticism, is not unfairly presented as strengthening the case which is being made out :

> I suppose Heaven is, through Eternity,
> The equalizing, ever and anon,
> In momentary rapture, great with small,
> Omniscience with intelligency, God
> With man,—the thunder-glow from pole to pole
> Abolishing, a blissful moment-space,
> Great cloud alike and small cloud, in one fire—
> As sure to ebb as sure again to flow
> When the new receptivity deserves
> The new completion. There's the Heaven for me.

The trend of the argument in 'A Death in the Desert' does not seem far removed from this. Man is at present

> Lower than God who knows all and can all,
> Higher than beasts which know and can so far
> As each beast's limit, perfect to an end,
> Nor conscious that they know, nor craving more;
> While man knows partly but conceives beside,
> Creeps ever on from fancies to the fact,
> And in this striving, this converting air
> Into a solid he may grasp and use,
> Finds progress, man's distinctive mark alone,
> Not God's and not the beasts' : God is, they are,
> Man partly is, and wholly hopes to be.

What is the answer to the question, 'What does man wholly hope to be'? If the answer be 'perfect man,' then have we not to find a new name for such a being ; or at least does not some other process begin there in the same way as the stage of 'perfect brute' is the beginning of a phase of life when the word brute will have to be abandoned ? One is tempted to understand Browning's belief to be that perfect humanity is divinity manifested as fully as human conditions will allow ; that humanity is not different from divinity in kind but in degree, or if we may venture so to express it, as humanity has developed from animal nature, so a new nature will develop from human nature, which, for want of a better term, we must call divine. So in ' Rabbi Ben Ezra ' (v.).

> Rejoice we are allied
> To That which doth provide
> And not partake, effect and not receive !
> A spark disturbs our clod ;
> Nearer we hold of God
> Who gives, than of His tribes that take, I must believe.

But how much nearer is seen in a following stanza (xiii.) :

> I summon age
> To grant youth's heritage,
> Life's struggle having so far reached its term :
> Thence shall I pass, approved
> A man, *for aye removed*
> *From the developed brute ; a god though in the germ.*

Nor does our poet in thought climb up only from man to God ; he climbs down from God to man. He sees not only the divinity of humanity, but the humanity of divinity. God may be a million things, and have a million activities of which man can know nothing. All we can truly perceive of God is what we see through our human eyes, and, though this is only part of the whole, yet we are not deceived as to its veracity. What we know of God is true though it be not the whole truth ; nor can any part of that greater whole deny the already known. Browning revels in the likeness of God and man.

> Why ever make man's good distinct from God's ;
> Or, finding they are one, why dare mistrust ?
>   ('Paracelsus.')

Humanity is never a negation of divinity, but rather an incomplete form of divinity. The virtues which constitute the perfect human do not have to be subtracted before that human can become divine ; nor is the reverse true, save in measure or quantity, never in quality. Man, we repeat, does not, for Browning, become equal with God. He must always be the product of that personality towards whose nature he is permitted to strive ; but he may rise to a state so far removed from manhood as brutehood is from manhood, call his ultimate—if it be this—what we will. This is a conclusion in which the mind can rest, and we think Browning's mind rested there. And, though no single passage warrants this conclusion, we think the cumulative effect of the passages quoted brings us there. This is an intelligible end to the aeonian growth of the human soul. We do not need to follow it further, for we are no longer following manhood. As Professor Herford says, in concluding his excellent book on Browning—the exception mentioned on p. 207—we see in his poetry ' man lifted by the law of love into a service which is perfect freedom, into *an approximation to God which is only the fullest realization of humanity.*' [1]

> What is left for us, save, in growth
> Of soul, to rise up, far past both,
> From the gift looking to the giver,
> And from the cistern to the river,
> And from the finite to infinity,
> And from man's dust to God's divinity ?
> ('Christmas Eve.')

As we have read Browning there is no inconsistency in the two conceptions of the life after death which contend together in his mind—that which sees it as a gradual continuation of slow progressive methods, and that which sees it as a state of complete transformation. May not the latter be the completion of the former ?

Nor is there any inconsistency of thought in the conception of the destiny of man, as just described, on the one hand, and the nature of Christ on the other ;

---
[1] Italics ours. We do not wish to go further than the connotation of these words ; but we would wish them to bear every ounce of meaning which they can be made to carry.

for Christ is always, for Browning, the miracle of God made man—not man so filled with God as to have become divine, but God made man, different in kind, not merely in degree.

There is an apparent inconsistency in the passionate earnestness of the poet in assuring us that the earth life is a moral probation, with his certainty of the ultimate triumph of good. Men say glibly enough that if everything is going to come right in the end why worry? This inconsistency is apparent rather than real. Two men can both be fully happy without being equally happy. The capacity for goodness or happiness is the decisive factor. It is that capacity which is determinable in the earth life; which is made or not made here.

10

The only point not yet considered in Browning's after-world is his conception of the communion of souls here and hereafter. (a) Does he believe that there can be communion here with those whom we call the dead?

We know his great mistrust of spiritualism and all it claimed, and one concludes from Mrs. Orr's *Life* that this was one of the few subjects on which he ever had any serious difference with his wife. The latter believed in spiritualism passionately, and was not even repelled by any 'manifestation,' however grotesque. Browning, on the other hand, 'absolutely denied the good faith of all the persons concerned'; and though he was in a more judicial frame of mind when he wrote 'Mr. Sludge the Medium,' 'in which he says everything which can excuse the liar, and, what is still more remarkable, modify the lie,' yet he remained 'subject for many years to gusts of uncontrollable emotion which would sweep over him whenever the question of "spirits" or "spiritualism" was revived... Mr.

Browning never denied the abstract possibility of spiritual communication with either living or dead; he only denied that such communication had ever been proved or that any useful end could be subserved by it.'[1]

There is a passage in 'Pauline' where Browning seems to long for the presence of the dead Shelley. But the *locus classicus* of this desired communion is the one in the Introduction to 'The Ring and the Book.' It is important enough to be fully quoted, and we have seen no exposition which satisfies us, and so have attempted one here.

> O lyric Love, half angel and half bird,
> And all a wonder and a wild desire,—
> Boldest of hearts that ever braved the sun,
> Took sanctuary within the holier blue,
> And sang a kindred soul out to his face,—
> Yet human at the red-ripe of the heart—
> When the first summons from the darkling earth
> Reached thee amid thy chambers, blanched their blue,
> And bared them of the glory—to drop down,
> To toil for man, to suffer or to die,—
> This is the same voice: can thy soul know change?
> Hail then, and hearken from the realms of help!
> Never may I commence my song, my due
> To God who best taught song by gift of thee,
> Except with bent head and beseeching hand—
> That still, despite the distance and the dark,
> What was, again may be; some interchange
> Of grace, some splendour once thy very thought,
> Some benediction anciently thy smile:
> —Never conclude, but raising hand and head
> Thither where eyes, that cannot reach, yet yearn
> For all hope, all sustainment, all reward,
> Their utmost up and on, so blessing back—
> In those thy realms of help, that heaven thy home,
> Some whiteness which, I judge, thy face makes proud,
> Some wanness where, I think, thy foot may fall!
>   (1391–1416.)

[1] Mrs. Sutherland Orr, *Life and Letters of Robert Browning*, pp. 209-11

There is, of course, little doubt that this passage, the 'posy' for the inside of his 'ring,' is an apostrophe to the poet's dead wife. When Nathaniel Hawthorne visited the Brownings in 1858 he described Mrs. Browning as 'a pale small person, scarcely embodied at all . . . sweetly disposed to the whole human race, though only remotely akin to it.' 'It is hardly possible,' says Canon Scott Holland,[1] 'but that those who remember her will not know a little more of what is to be felt moving under the great lines, "O lyric Love," &c. The fluttering passion of the bird, with the white, flashing purity of the angel, the wonder, strangeness, delight of a visitant presence, caught and held in the body for a space, for our joy, and released to fly back in a rush to the home that was hers all along, leaving to us the sense of swift passage, as of a bird through a world that could not hold her, so that we are left startled out of our humdrum selves, knowing that we have entertained an angel unawares.'

Our interpretation of the passage is as follows : The loved one always belonged to a higher kind of existence. She dwelt apart in a holier blue, not since her death only, but always. Shrouded in that house of mystery in Wimpole Street, always secluded in a sick-room, and, moreover, dwelling in a 'holier blue,' in a more profound glory of inspiration, than the poet ever knew. She was always a kindred soul to the sun, and like a skylark (? 'half bird') sang, braving its very face. Yet she was no inhuman being. She had written of

Some Pomegranate, which, if cut deep down the middle,
Shows a heart within, blood tinctured, of a veined humanity ;

and she herself is 'red-ripe of the heart.'

The poet imagines her in some glorious life before this human existence. Yet the needs of earth had called her and she had answered the summons ; though

[1] *Some Hawarden Letters*, p. 185, quoted in Cook's *Commentary on 'The Ring and the Book.'*

the glory of that upper world had been lessened, its blue blanched, by her coming, when she came to toil for man, to suffer, and to die. Probably concurrently with this thought the poet has deliberately blended that of her seclusion in her home before he knew her, and her response to his own need when she left the sanctuary of inspiration, impoverishing her family, and came to serve him in less conducive tasks.

He pleads that his voice is still the same, and surely she cannot have changed. So now even when she has passed to heaven, whence all man's help is derived, will she not respond to his need? God taught him to sing by giving her to him. She is the dynamic and motive of his inspiration. His song is his due to God in return for His gift to her. He vows he will never begin any poem without lifting his heart and hand to her in prayer for a renewal of inspiration; so that, in spite of the distance and the dark,

> What was, again may be; some interchange
> Of grace, some splendour once thy very thought,
> Some benediction anciently thy smile.

Nor will he ever finish a poem without his whole soul going out to her in yearning for encouragement and help and reward, even though his eyes, strain as they may, ' their utmost up and on,' can no longer see her.

She has given him her blessing. He in return blesses her, even in the realms whence help is dispensed, the heaven which is now her home; blessing both the spiritual part of her nature incident to her new and heavenly life, the whiteness or radiance of heaven which is proud to be manifested in such a face; blessing also the still human part of her nature, which ensures his recognition of her, the wanness of his dear invalid wife, by which he will still know her as his own, however she may progress in that spiritual existence, wherever among the heights of heaven her foot may fall. He gives her his blessing—as she gives hers to him—because, although she has entered a new life clothed in the white radiance of a heavenly existence, she still retains traces of her humanity in the wanness of her look, so that though she is 'half angel,' though she walks upon heights to which at present he cannot climb, yet wherever her foot may fall she will bear marks that will lead him to her, and he will know her for his own, his lyric love, 'half angel,' but also still 'half bird.'

In this longing of the poet we note the same desire for communion rather than communication which we saw in Tennyson. Browning does not desire the latter. He revels in the sense of presence, in a linking of spirit too full and deep for word or smile.

(b) Concerning the reunion and communion of souls after death the poet has more to say to us. He recognizes that reunion after death follows from the identity of the soul then with the soul in this life. If it is true of all souls to say,

> From first to last of lodging, I was I,
> And not at all the place that harboured me,[1]

then we must be capable of recognizing and rejoining, in a further existence, those whom we knew and loved in this. We need not hesitate to say that after his wife's death the idea of a rapturous reunion became very precious to Browning. 'For himself,' says Professor Herford, 'death was now inseparably intertwined with all that he had known of love, and the prospect of the supreme reunion which death, as he believed, was to bring him drew it nearer to the core of his imagination and passion.'

In 'Red Cotton Nightcap Country' reunion is hinted at:

> O friend! who makest warm my wintry world,
> And wise my heaven, if there we consort too;

[1] 'Prince Hohenstiel-Schwangau.'

but it bursts out more fully in 'Prospice.' Here the joy of anticipated reunion takes all the sting away from death. He is glad to pay

> life's arrears
> Of pain, darkness, and cold.
> For sudden the worst turns the best to the brave,
> The black minute's at end,
> And the elements' rage, the fiend-voices that rave,
> Shall dwindle, shall blend,
> Shall change, shall become first a peace out of pain,
> Then a light, then thy breast,
> O thou soul of my soul! I shall clasp thee again,
> And with God be the rest!

The lines that Browning wrote on seeing Leighton's picture are very close to this idea. Leighton depicts the scene where Eurydice the wife of Orpheus is allowed to depart from Hades, since the heart of Pluto has been deeply moved by Orpheus's playing. The condition of her release, however, is that Eurydice shall follow behind Orpheus and that the latter shall not turn back to see if she is following. He turns before he reaches earth and so loses her for ever. The longing for reunion is heard in Browning's 'Eurydice to Orpheus'

> But give them me, the mouth, the eyes, the brow!
> Let them once more absorb me! . . .
> . . . .
> Hold me but safe again within the bond
> Of one immortal look.

Perhaps there is no more beautiful passage in the English language touching the desire for reunion of souls after death than the closing stanza of 'Evelyn Hope.' She was a beautiful girl of sixteen. Her lover was thrice her age, but her time to love had not come when

> God's hand beckoned unawares,—
> And the sweet white brow is all of her.

Yet, through all the years, and possibly 'more lives yet,' he will wait and love. How can he make her know, when she wakes in heaven, that he loves her, has always loved her?

> I loved you, Evelyn, all the while.
> My heart seemed full as it could hold?
> There was place and to spare for the frank young smile,
> And the red young mouth, and the hair's young gold.
> So, hush,—I will give you this leaf to keep:
> See, I shut it inside the sweet cold hand!
> There, that is our secret: go to sleep!
> You will wake, and remember, and understand.

VI

CONCLUSION

VI

CONCLUSION

WE have now traced the idea of immortality throughout the works of the more important poets of the nineteenth century. We have tried to accompany those poets as they soared to the heights of vision and gazed into the country beyond the horizon. As we meditate on what we have seen through their eyes we have to confess that the best-known fact about this country is that it is still unknown. Until we make the journey for ourselves, the land beyond the horizon must always be to some extent the unknown.

At the same time, portions of the landscape light up for us as we view them through the eyes of those who, among men, have seen most clearly through the mists of mortality. Wordsworth—to use a phrase of Olive Schreiner's—' gathers light out of the past to shed it on the future.' Valleys of deep gloom, from the depths of which we seem to hear the cries of men in despair, are filled with sunlight and bird-song by the magic of Shelley's laughter; and we recall another sentence of Olive Schreiner: ' The echoes of despair slunk away, for the laugh of a brave, strong heart is death to them.' In Tennyson we hear the cry of a man who has sounded the depths of human fear at the thought of death. ' It is a cry that mingles with the mystery of wide spaces, of sullen sunsets or of sodden dawns; the cry of a child lost at night-time; the cry of some stricken creature in the dark ';[1] yet that cry receives its answer ' from that high land ' though it be ' in a tongue no

---

[1] *Tennyson*, Harold Nicolson, p. 302.

man could understand'; and behind the distant mountains of that 'undiscover'd country'

> God made Himself an awful rose of Dawn.

When we are with Arnold and Clough the mists sometimes roll heavily between us and the land of the hereafter; and when we are with Swinburne we wonder whether it exists at all.

Browning takes us farthest and shows us most. He does not attempt to give us a speculative map of the country beyond. Rather, from the heights of vision he tells us what he sees. And no poet of the century, we think, saw so clearly or so far. He sees men struggling still, but struggle is assured of victory. Jungle on earth has become woodland in heaven. Storm-tossed oceans have become quiet seas that mirror cloudless skies. Friends, united, lift their eyes to yet greater heights. With almost bated breath we ask our prophet what these heights may be. But concerning them even he can tell us little. He lifts his hand and points, almost in silence. Our gaze follows his finger. There, in the far, far distance, are lonely peaks of snow-clad purity standing out against the blue. They are the 'other heights'; the goal of a humanity which has become at last divine; an abode where God can be known in yet greater fullness; where joy and fellowship, love and harmony, truth and beauty, reign eternally, and where, beyond all human voices, there is peace.

INDEX

A

'ADONAIS,' 71
Aeschylus, 87
Aristotle, 15, 25
  Quoted, 20
Arnold, Matthew, Ch. IV. (1), 144, 224
  Quoted, 17, 53, 78, Ch. IV. (1)
Arnold, Dr., 150
Athanasius, quoted, 207
Atheism, 48, 54 ff., 160, 178
Atonement, doctrine of, 149, 180
Aurelius, Marcus, 128, 130

B

BANVILLE, THEODORE DE, 164
Baudelaire, Charles, 166
Beaumont, 38
Benson, A. C., quoted, 82 ff.
Bradley, A.C., 102, 119, 120
Brown, Professor William, 45
Browning, Robert, 13, 16, 18, 21, 161, Ch. V., 224
  Quoted, 22, 49, 54, 77, Ch. V.
Browning, Mrs., 175, 178, 193, 198, 214, 216 ff.
Buchanan, Robert, 177
Bunyan, 20
Burne-Jones, 163
Burns, quoted, 15
Burton, Sir Richard, 163
Byron, 56, 69, 154, 178
  Quoted, 15

C

CAMPBELL, MRS. OLWEN WARD, 14
Carlyle, quoted, 21, 181

Chesterton, G. K., quoted, 18, 176, 187
Chopin, 18
Clough, 125, Ch. IV. (2), 154, 224
  Quoted, Ch. IV. (2)
Coleridge, 34, 37, 38, 41
  Quoted, 14, 69
Cook, A. C., quoted, 177

D

DARWIN, 90 ff.
Dowden, Professor, quoted, 15, 50, 180, 187
Dreams, 24, 28, 68

E

EDGERTON-SMITH, MISS, 188
Eliot, George, quoted, 36
Emerson, quoted, 23
Euripides, 87
Evolution, theory of, 89 ff.

F

FEELING, PLACE OF, IN ARRIVING AT TRUTH, 25 ff.
Fontanes, quoted, 132
Fox, 35

G

GALLOWAY, DR. G., 84
Garrod, 38, 39
Gladstone, quoted, 102, 127
Goethe, quoted, 15, 128, 141, 142

INDEX

Gosse, Edmund, quoted, 154, 156, 167
Graham, James Norman, 164
Green, T. H., 153

H

HALLAM, 85, 86, 101 *ff.*
Harper, Professor, quoted, 22, 34
Harrison, Frederic, 127
   Quoted, 133
Hawthorne, Nathaniel, quoted, 216
Hazlitt, quoted, 53
Hegel, 87
Hell, 50, 57 *ff.*, 111, 112, 180, 203 *ff.*
Hell Complex, 58, 67
Herford, Professor, 183
   Quoted, 177, 185, 199, 213, 218
Herrick, quoted, 14
Herschel, 92
Holland, Canon Scott, quoted, 216
Home, 175
Homer, 87
Hugo, Victor, 157, 162, 163, 170
   Quoted, 174
Hunt, John and Leigh, 51
Hutton, R. H., quoted, 134
Huxley, 111
Hypnotism, 45

I

INFLUENCE, IMMORTALITY OF, 36
'In Memoriam,' exposition of, 101
Isaiah, quoted, 22

J

JONES, PROFESSOR HENRY, quoted, 161
Jonson, Ben, 102
Jowett, 87

K

KANT, 86
Keats, 71
   Quoted, 17, 20, 28
Kingsley, 53

L

LAMB, CHARLES, quoted, 20, 53
Landor, 159, 162, 164
Lecky, W. E. H., quoted, 96
Leighton, 219
Lightfoot, Bishop, 95
Linton, Mrs. Lynn, 164
Longfellow, quoted, 23
Lowell, James Russell, quoted, 25

M

MACKINTOSH, PROFESSOR H. R., 84
Marston, P. B., 159, 163, 164
Maurice, 92
Mazzini, 157, 163, 170
Milton, 29, 163
   Quoted, 22
Moffatt, Professor, 127
Morley, Lord, quoted, 56
Mormons, 14
Morris, William, 163
Mozart, 23
Mustard, Professor, 88
Myers, F. W. H., quoted, 37

N

NATIONS, LEAGUE OF, 90
Newman, 149
Nicolson, Harold, quoted, 223

O

'ODE ON THE INTIMATIONS OF IMMORTALITY,' 37 *ff.*
Origen, 46
Original goodness, doctrine of, 45

INDEX

Original sin, doctrine of, 45
Orr, Mrs. Sutherland, quoted, 193, 214
Owen, 92

P

PANTHEISM, 72 ff., 85, 86, 89, 137, 160, 168, 186, 207
Patmore, Coventry, quoted, 86
Paul, Herbert, quoted, 127
Plato, 37 ff., 74 ff., 86 ff., 141, 142
Poetry, didactic, 15, 16, 101, 188
Polidori, quoted, 69
Polytheism, 160, 208
Pre-existence, doctrine of, 39 ff., 87
Prescott, quoted, 28
Psychology, 23, 45, 58, 174

R

RATIONALISM, 126 ff.
Reminiscence, doctrine of, 39, 45, 75
Renan, quoted, 136
Resurrection, doctrine of the, 83, 108, 193
Reul, Paul de, quoted, 170
'Ring and the Book,' The, Introduction analysed, 215 ff.
Robertson, 92
Rossetti, Christina, 155
Rousseau, 45
Ruskin, 127
Russell, G. W. E., quoted, 128

S

SADHU SUNDAR SINGH, 20
Saffi, Aurelio, 163
St. Francis of Assisi, 20
St. John, Revelation of, 20
St. Mark, quoted, 26
Saintsbury, Professor, 133
Schiller, F. C. S., quoted, 84
Schreiner, Olive, quoted, 223
Sedgwick, 92
Shairp, Principal, quoted, 133

Shakespeare, 163, 173
Quoted, 24
Shelley, Ch. II., 81, 128, 142, 163, 178
Quoted, 19, 20, 23, 24, Ch. II.
Shelley, Harriet, 51 ff.
Shelley, Mary, 51 ff.
Sidney, Sir Philip, 102
Souls, Communion of, 117 ff., 214 ff.
Southey, 54
Spiritualism, 14, 121, 175, 214
Stevenson, quoted, 21, 182
Stoicism, 127 ff.
Swinburne, 14, 125, Ch. IV. (3), 224
Quoted, Ch. IV. (3)
Syllogism, 27, 104
Symonds, J. A., quoted, 151

T

TENNYSON, 21, Ch. III., 125, 143, 153, 155, 163, 174, 197, 218, 223
Quoted, 18, 21, 40, Ch. III., 200
Tennyson, Hallam, quoted, 95
Thomas, Edward, quoted, 155
Thompson, Francis, quoted, 77
Trelawney, 163
Quoted, 56
Trinity, doctrine of, 142
Truth, how arrived at by the poet, 19 ff.
Turner, 18
Twain, Mark, 97
Tyndall, 92, 111

U

UNIVERSALISM, THEORY OF, 114 185, 200, 206

V

VEGETARIANS, 14
Vere, Aubrey de, 111
Voltaire, 22

W

Waddington, Samuel, quoted, 150
Watts, 16
Watts-Dunton, Clara, quoted, 156
Webster, John, 163

Wordsworth, Ch. II., 81, 223
  Quoted, 16, 21, 22, 26, 29, 30, Ch. II.
Wordsworth, Dora, 34
Wordsworth, Dorothy, 34, 41